AMOROUS
NIGHTMARES
OF DELAY

PAJ BOOKS

BONNIE MARRANCA AND GAUTAM DASGUPTA

SERIES EDITORS

FRANK O'HARA

AMOROUS NIGHTMARES OF DELAY

SELECTED PLAYS

THE JOHNS HOPKINS UNIVERSITY PRESS
BALTIMORE AND LONDON

Originally published as *Selected Plays* in 1978 by Full Court Press
Johns Hopkins Paperbacks edition, 1997
06 05 04 03 02 01 00 99 98 97   5 4 3 2 1

The Johns Hopkins University Press
2715 North Charles Street
Baltimore, Maryland 21218-4319
The Johns Hopkins Press Ltd., London

Acknowledgments: "The General" was originally published in *Arts & Literature*, Number 4, Lausanne, Switzerland; it was also published in *Eight Plays from Off-Off Broadway*, edited by Nick Orzel and Michael Smith, 1966 (Bobbs-Merrill). "Try, Try!" was published in *Artists' Theatre*, edited by Herbert Machiz, 1960 (Grove Press). "Awake in Spain," was published in *The Hasty Papers*, "Flight 115" was originally published in the anonymous issue of *Adventures in Poetry*. The Coronation Murder Mystery © 1978 John Ashbery, Kenneth Koch, and Frank O'Hara. Reprinted by permission of Georges Borchardt, Inc. for John Ashbery.

CAUTION: Professionals and amateurs are hereby warned that TRY! TRY!, being fully protected by copyright, is subject to royalties. For all performing rights in this play, including professional, amateur, motion picture, recitation, lecturing, public reading, radio and television broadcasting, and right of translation into foreign languages, application should be made to Samuel French, Inc. 25 West 45th Street, New York, N.Y. 10036.

ISBN 0-8018-5529-2 (pbk.)

Library of Congress Cataloging-in-Publication data will be found at the end of this book.

A catalog record for this book is available from the British Library.

CONTENTS

Preface to the 1997 Edition

In 1976, when Joan Simon, Anne Waldman, and I came up with the idea of publishing Frank O'Hara's plays at Full Court Press, our fledgling publishing venture, we envisaged a modest selection of perhaps 96 pages. But when the manuscripts began to arrive, we saw that there were a lot more plays than we had thought and that even the most "fugitive" items contained brilliant and irresistible passages. Thus this collection grew to its present size.

The book goes beyond expectations in other ways, as well. Frank O'Hara moved easily among the worlds of theater, dance, poetry, and art. Thus it is no coincidence that his plays tended to be produced by companies that combined genres, such as the American Theatre for Poets and the Artists' Theatre in New York, and the Poets Theatre in Cambridge, Massachusetts. In fact, his plays are more like poems in which characters materialize than like plays in which the traditional elements of plot and characterization predominate, and which must be staged to be most effective. O'Hara's plays are rare in that they are equally pleasurable on the stage and on the page.

It is with this cross-fertilization in mind that we include several untitled fragments and plays that could justifiably be classified as poems, film scripts, or interior monologues. In his plays as well as his poetry, O'Hara pushed the traditional limits of genres, enlarging their territories to make room for a larger and more complex human spirit. That expansiveness influenced our editorial policy.

Simon, Waldman, and I made a few changes in the manuscript versions of these plays. We corrected typographical errors and the few misspellings, keeping, however, the intentional misspellings. We aimed for consistency in capitalization, punctuation, and styling within each play, again except when it was obvious that a deviation from standard practice was intentional. In a few cases we inserted words that had been omitted from the manuscript, owing, no doubt, to haste in typing; these insertions appear in brackets. Some of the manuscripts we worked from seem to be first drafts, typed in a burst of inspiration and then dropped into a desk drawer. O'Hara had a casual attitude toward his manuscripts, but he also approved of tidying them up for publication.

The sequence of plays in this volume is roughly chronological, with variations that we feel make for a nicer "read" if one were to go straight through, which is tempting in a case such as this.

A great debt of gratitude is owed to all those who helped in the preparation of this volume. Maureen O'Hara, Frank's sister and the executrix of his estate, was as helpful and encouraging as possible. Donald Allen, whose editorial work on O'Hara's poetry is legendary, was of inestimable value in gathering manuscripts and background material. Joseph LeSueur was generous in writing an introduction that is as informative, intimate, and conversational as its subject, and in providing detailed information and good general advice, as was Bill Berkson, who also supplied documentary materials. Bill, Kenneth Koch, John Ashbery, Steven Rivers, Larry Rivers, and Frank Lima gave their enthusiastic approval for use of the plays they had written with Frank. Others were generous with their time and advice: Alex Smith, John Herbert McDowell, Alan Feldman, Ted Greenwald, Pat Padgett, Edward Gorey, Meredith Chutter, Larry Rivers, Tony Towle, and the staff of the Museum of Modern Art.

I would also like to acknowledge the various publications in which some of these plays appeared: "Awake in Spain" in *The Hasty Papers*, edited by Alfred Leslie; the second version of "TRY! TRY!" in *Artists Theatre*, edited by Herbert Machiz and published by Grove Press; "The General Returns from One Place to Another," originally published in *Art & Literature*, edited by John Ashbery, Anne Dunn, Rodrigo Moynihan, and Sonia Orwell, and reprinted in *Eight Off-Off Broadway Plays*, edited by Nick Orzel and Michael Smith and published by

Bobbs Merrill; and "Flight 115" in the special anonymous issue of *Adventures in Poetry,* edited by Larry Fagin. I would also like to point out that the Full Court Press edition of these plays was supported by a grant from the Literature Program of the National Endowment for the Arts.

Frank O'Hara's plays are fun to read because they are exhilarating, witty, and dreamy, and so it is a great pleasure to see them made available again for a new audience.

Ron Padgett
New York, 1996

Introduction to the 1997 Edition

During the period between the original publication of *Selected Plays* in 1978 and this new edition almost twenty years later, Frank O'Hara's fame as innovative poet, culture hero, and charismatic *animateur* grew so dramatically that his place in American letters now seems secure. But those years saw something else: unmistakable signs that he was on the way to becoming a legend.

Earlier, in the years immediately after his untimely death in 1966, there was a flurry of interest and activity inspired by his life and work. To some extent, that was to be expected; O'Hara was a poet with a cult following who died relatively young, at the age of forty. As time went on, however, one would have expected a dramatic falling off in the deluge of readings, panel discussions, concerts, art exhibitions, and celebrations in his honor.

That has not been the case. On the contrary, what was once a cottage industry has grown into a one-man literary movement lionizing someone who, in a way, is more alive now than in his lifetime—one of the sure signs of a legend in the making. If further evidence is desired, consider the following:

In commemoration of O'Hara's death, elaborate celebrations and memorials have been held in New York City every ten years—in 1976, 1986, and 1996—and there is every indication that the practice will continue. In addition, there have been frequent marathon readings of O'Hara's work, the most recent being an afternoon of poetry and music held at the Knitting Factory in lower Manhattan. Another notable occasion was the 1990 round robin reading of his long, surreal poem "Second Avenue" at St. Mark's Church.

A revised edition of the 1971 *Collected Poems* was published by the University of California Press in 1995; a new printing of *Meditations in an Emergency* appeared in 1996; after more than thirty years, *Lunch Poems* is still in print; and plans are afoot for new editions of *Love Poems (Tentative Title)* and *Poems Retrieved.* His poems also appear in numerous anthologies and are quoted regularly in reviews, articles, and books.

Brad Gooch's biography, *City Poet: The Life and Times of Frank O'Hara,* was published in 1993. It received widespread critical attention including a long, influential, profilelike review in the *New Yorker* that ranks O'Hara as a leading cultural figure. Earlier, in 1990, the University of Michigan Press published *Frank O'Hara: To Be True to a City,* a compilation of forty-six reviews and essays having to do with O'Hara.

In the 1980s, university art galleries and museums began mounting shows with O'Hara as their focal point. At the Skidmore College Art Gallery, there was an exhibit of *Oranges*, paintings by Grace Hartigan to poems by O'Hara, and at the William Benton Museum of Art at the University of Connecticut, Storrs, "Art with the Touch of a Poet" was offered in conjunction with an O'Hara conference and series of readings. Both the Whitney Museum of American Art and the Museum of Modern Art honored O'Hara with exhibitions shortly after his death.

Beginning in the 1980s, a new generation of American composers took up where Leonard Bernstein, Ned Rorem, Virgil Thomson, Morton Feldman, and Lukas Foss left off; like their distinguished predecessors, they set O'Hara's poetry to music. Chief among them is the prize-winning composer Ricky Ian Gordon.

In Britain, two TV documentaries about O'Hara's life and work were produced: one for the BCC in 1995 and another for Channel 4, London, in 1996. Meanwhile, O'Hara's own film, *The Last Clean Shirt,* a collaboration with the painter Alfred Leslie, was part of the 1995 Beat Culture Exhibition at the Whitney Museum. The NET documentary on O'Hara, made in his lifetime, continues to be shown regularly.

In 1987, next to several lines by Walt Whitman, a quotation from O'Hara's long poem "Meditations in an Emergency" was inscribed in bold brass letters on the plaza fence of New York City's Battery Park. A few years later, a plaque was placed on the building at 90 University Place, designating it as the poet's residence from 1957 to 1958.

In July 1996, a "Manhattan Poetry Map" was published by Poets House that shows two of the four apartments where O'Hara lived, at 441 East 9th Street and at 791 Broadway; along with Whitman, Emerson, Elizabeth Bishop, and William Carlos Williams, O'Hara is prominently quoted on the map.

On January 20, 1994, O'Hara made his first appearance in a *New York Times* crossword puzzle. The clue: "*Lunch Poems* poet."

His gravesite at the Green River Cemetery in East Hampton, New York, has become a shrine, where flowers, New York City Ballet tickets, coins, seashells, and various talismans are left anonymously over the years.

Finally, the plays: In 1979, the well-known collaborator of Stephen Sondhein, James Lapine, directed "Awake in Spain" at the Manhattan Theater Club; the next year, the celebrated avant-garde director Peter Sellars staged five verse plays by O'Hara at La Mama E.T.C.; and O'Hara's most frequently performed and best known plays, "Try! Try!" and "The General Returns From One Place to Another" were presented in a number of staged readings.

There is more to be said, but I believe my point has been made. As for the plays, one hopes that in the future these original and scintillating theater works of Frank O'Hara will be more widely produced. Perhaps this new edition of his plays will help bring that about.

Joe LeSueur
New York, 1996

Introduction

In the *Big Sky* "Homage to Frank O'Hara" number, Ruth Krauss tells us that one of the things Frank taught her at his New School poetry workshop was: "You call it something—i.e., a play—and everyone will accept it as such." Here's something else. In a letter to James Broughton, Frank confesses that "*What Century?* might appear to most people to be unstageable" but that "I see it on a stage." I guess we should take Frank at his word on both counts, though it seems to me he's asking for a lot. Right off, the stage directions for *What Century?* call for "waves breaking like bees on the shelf of Armorica, while the scent of burning almond leaves fills the nippled sky"; and later, "a helicopter alights in a field where some Creoles are smoking opium and complaining." Posing an entirely different challenge to anyone undertaking its production is *Flight 115*, the Bill Berkson collaboration; this time we have neither stage directions nor a cast of characters, only a dialogue of sorts presumably between two people. Maybe what Kenneth Koch said to me some years ago is more to the point. He described Frank's plays—and his own, no doubt—as "literary comments."

In deciding to include eclogues in this volume, the Full Court Press would appear to have been influenced by Frank's unexacting notions about what constitutes a play. Another guideline might have been the fact that at least one eclogue, *Amorous Nightmares of Delay*, was clearly written for the stage. In any event, it's a decision I won't quarrel with any more than I'd fault the inclusion of *Act & Portrait* and *Love on the Hoof*. Both are film scripts, highly unconventional ones at that, and I assume they're being offered in much the same spirit as the eclogues.

The General Returns from One Place to Another is probably Frank's most accessible play; it happens also to be my favorite. Billed with LeRoi Jones's *The Baptism,* it ran for a week or so at a small downtown theater—on East Fourth Street, as I recall. General MacArthur was gravely ill at the time (he died a month later), and there was actually something in the press about the tastelessness of satirizing the great man. Otherwise, not much notice was taken of the play; I remember Harold Clurman, in *The Nation,* giving *The Baptism* a largely favorable review without mentioning *The General.* (LeRoi was suddenly hot because of the sensation created by *Dutchman.*) Frank couldn't have cared less. What he did care about was the lovely performance Taylor Mead gave; he liked it so much that he added Taylor's name to the play's dedication, which eventually became "To Vincent Warren and to Warner Brothers and Taylor Mead."

Ideally, *The General* should move at a brisker pace than the performance it received back in 1964. Written in the form of blackouts, it never presses its points or tries for laughs in the manner of a farce. Nor does it have the bite of real satire: it is too good-natured, too low-keyed. I still haven't given up hope that someday it will be revived—with Taylor, of course, back as the general. A snappy musical score would enhance the proceedings, and I see a Margaret Dumont-type as Mrs. Forbes. Couple the play with John Ashbery's *The Heroes* (Kenward Elmslie's inspired idea) and we'd have a terrific evening in the theater.

Just as he avoided talking about his childhood, Frank never in the nine and a half years I lived with him talked about what he did in the war. Yet he would listen to, and even encourage me to go on about, my own childhood and wartime experiences. Not surprisingly, this response to the past was carried over into his writing. But in *Try! Try!* we have something of an exception. Offhand, I can think of only two other works of his that touch on World War II: *Lament and Chastisement,* an autobiographical prose piece written about a year earlier for a creative writing course at Harvard, and his "Ode to Michael Goldberg ('s Birth and Other Births)," which evokes his childhood as well. Note, too, that *Try! Try!* has an intensity and cynicism not found in his other plays and a basically realistic situation equally uncharacteristic.

The first *Try! Try!* has been produced only once, in 1951, at the Poets' Theater in Cambridge, Mass. (It was on a bill with three other one-acters, by John Ashbery, Richard Eberhardt and Lyon Phelps.) I recently asked Hal Fondren, one of Frank's roommates and best friends at Harvard, how he liked it. What he recalled most vividly was a small scandal for which he was chiefly responsible. Unlike most members of the audience, he found many individual lines hilarious and saw no reason to suppress his laughter. At the end of the performance, an irate Thornton Wilder rose from his seat and, looking straight at Hal, sternly rebuked members of the audience who had laughed; he pointed out that what they had just seen was a serious work, possibly an important one. Frank probably never had a more unlikely champion. He was doing graduate work at the University of Michigan at the time and never saw the production.

The second version has been produced twice in New York, in 1953 and in 1968; both productions were downtown, and neither of them can remotely be described as a commercial venture. And one summer—memory suggests it was 1965—Shirley King, Larry Rivers and Syd Solomon got together and performed it in Ann Roiphe's backyard in East Hampton, just for the fun of it. There was also a performance of sorts that never saw opening night, a reading Frank planned to give with Gaby Rodgers on a bill with three plays by Kenneth Koch, Elaine May and Arnold Weinstein. That was in 1958, I think. Convinced that the others felt his play would reduce their chances of having a success, Frank had me come to a preview performance to help him decide what to do. I advised him to withdraw, not just because he found the atmosphere strained but also because I thought what he and Gaby were doing wasn't theatrical enough. So *Four by Four,* the original overall title, became *Three by Three.* Frank characteristically took all of this in his stride, without rancor; I think he was even sorry when the show closed after a few performances.

Those two New York productions of *Try! Try!* were quite dissimilar. The first one, which Herbert Machiz directed, was given a charged, heady performance dominated by Anne Meacham, who had a chilling way with the part of Violet. Directing the play some fifteen years later, Ann MacIntosh took a somewhat different tack: she found irony, rather than intense drama, in the play's soap opera-like situation and made the proceedings almost light-hearted by comparison. And this time around, there was no way the actress playing Violet could dominate the performance, for John was played by Frederick Forrest, an immensely attractive, talented actor who has since done interesting things in TV and films. How Frank would have loved him! The play, incidentally, was performed alone in 1968; instead of presenting it with one or two other things, MacIntosh arranged to have various poets read from Frank's works at each of the ten or so performances.

Frank wrote a good number of these plays in fairly haphazard fashion, whether by himself or in collaboration. At least that's my impression—and not just from the way the plays read, either. Specifically, I remember how two lines found their way into one of the more surrealist works. One Saturday afternoon—this was at the 49th Street apartment, in 1953, two years before I moved in—Bill Weaver and I were sitting around with Frank, who was busy at his typewriter and talking to us at the same time. Bill had brought Frank a half-pint of brandy; he asked me if I wanted some, and I said I'd rather have a cognac. "Didn't you know cognac was brandy, queenie?" Bill shot back. Frank laughed and promptly put what Bill said into the play. A little later, he happened to remember a line from an anecdote Bill de Kooning had recently told him over drinks at the Cedar Bar. "It's terrible under Kay Francis's armpits," de Kooning quoted Arshile Gorky as saying to him as they were leaving one of her movies. That, too, went into the play he would call *Awake in Spain*. (Gorky's weird observation was a source of continued amusement to Frank; ten years later, the line popped up again in a poem called "On Rachmaninoff's Birthday & About Arshile Gorky.")

Some of these plays, then, might be regarded as dadaistic, as part of the surrealist tradition, or as the verbal equivalent of aleatory music (frankly, though it's unimportant, I'm not sure how they should be categorized). At the same time, about half of the works in this volume, some of the more far-out ones too, are either eclogues or Noh plays. Of course in his treatment of these traditional forms Frank was playing with conventions, much the way he did in some of his poetry. Presumably, with the exception of *Amorous Nightmares of Delay,* the eclogues weren't written for the stage; but the other works were, and I think there's no question that at least three of them would strike most theater people as unplayable, line by line, and unstageable as a whole. Jimmy Waring, a dancer-choreographer who died a few years ago, solved the various problems these plays pose by not dealing with them—and did wonders with *Awake in Spain* simply by having the actors sit at a table, with a narrator giving stage directions and identifying the many characters.

But what is the key to *staging* these more problematic plays? As with Kenward Elmslie's marvelously original *City Junket,* any director and group of actors intent on bringing alive *Awake in Spain, Change Your Bedding!* and *A Day in the Life of the Czar* must discover a subtext—not merely effective bits of business (even the most conventional plays demand that kind of invention) but also a line of action that supports the speeches in theatrical terms and treats them as ordinary language, not as poetry. Or is there another way of approaching these plays? Let's hope we'll have the chance to see a fully staged *City Junket,* for which Bill Elliott is now writing music: its production would very likely show the way.

After reading these unconventional works, one might conclude that Frank couldn't have had much interest in the kind of plays that appeal to large audiences. Which means, now that I think about it, he would have been in the company of every other poet I've known over the years. Not that I'm reproaching them; I think it's easy to see why poets might not like popular theater. For I can imagine that its use of language would strike them as deplorable, since it has nothing to do with what they're up to; and partly what they're up to is having total control, a creative situation playwrights obviously can't have. But Frank, it seems to me, was different. He didn't even complain about O'Neill's language, which I've heard more than one poet disparage. (Though of course it was O'Neill's tragic vision that drew him to those late plays.) And when he had a play done, he never interfered or worried that his lines would be tampered with. "I'm just grateful they're doing it," he said when I suggested he be more assertive during the rehearsal period of one of his plays. (I feel sure that Diane di Prima, Alan Marlowe, John Myers or anybody else connected with the productions of his plays would support me on this. I also remember how much Herbert Machiz wanted to work with Frank again after doing *Try! Try!*) To get back to his attitude towards professional bigtime theater: without wanting to write for it, he gave the impression that he was more excited by certain Broadway plays than by a lot of things he saw downtown. Even if he disliked something on the order of *The Dark at the Top of the Stairs,* which I made the mistake of taking him to after believing a rave review in the *Times,* he seemed not to find the experience as painful as sitting through a ponderous and arty Lionel Abel play about the race problem we'd seen the previous season.

I'd like to extend this digression, because I think some readers might be curious about what plays Frank liked. Stanley Kauffmann, who used to be the *Times* drama critic, raised this very question at a P.E.N.-sponsored symposium on Frank's work a year or so ago. "Oh, Frank liked everything," answered a member of the panel. Not so, though I can understand how somebody might entertain such a notion. After all, didn't he go for trashy movies? (He saw Linda Darnell and Tab Hunter in *Island of Desire* three times, and *Rhapsody* with Elizabeth Taylor he liked so much that he titled a poem after it.) Another reason why Frank was misunderstood in this respect had to do with his enthusiasm, which a lot of the time was taken for permissiveness. He wanted to like everything, plays included, and for him this meant focusing almost exclusively on positive aspects of a work. As a result, he could be unreliable when he described something he'd seen, heard or read; and he was so supportive, so reluctant to come down hard on anybody's honest efforts, that he inevitably seemed uncritical.

So what plays did he like? By and large, as I've indicated, not the kind he wrote: plays in the realistic tradition were mainly what he seemed to prefer. And the ones I remember his being moved by, all of them solid works, hardly justify the assertion that "Frank liked everything": *In the Summer House, The Iceman Cometh, Long Day's Journey Into Night, Hughie, Strange Interlude* (the Actors Studio revival), *Look Back in Anger, Inadmissible Evidence, A Taste of Honey, I Am a Camera, The Member of the Wedding,* and *Who's Afraid of Virginia Woolf?* The off-Broadway productions of Chekhov, Ibsen and Strindberg should also be mentioned. So should the avant-garde theater: he was enthusiastic about many things done by Judson Church, the Living Theater and the Artists' Theater—and *ecstatic* about everything he ever saw by Samuel Beckett. Of Beckett's plays, *Happy Days* must have been his favorite; he saw it three, maybe four times.

Three more digressions:

1) I never knew anybody who disliked critics more than Frank did. I know that my brief stint as a theater reviewer for *The Village Voice* didn't exactly thrill him. "Don't be so mean," he told me once. "If you can't say anything good about a play, don't review it." I reminded him that I didn't get paid unless I turned in a review, at which point he changed the subject—without letting me off the hook, of course. (See his poem "The Bores," which was inspired by John Simon.)

2) Here's how Frank's enthusiasm, the way he tried to like everything, could get the better of him. After we saw the decidedly mediocre *Sweet Bird of Youth,* which was only partially redeemed by Geraldine Page's bravura performance, he got on the horn to Patsy Southgate and gave her such an exciting description of the play that she rushed out for tickets the next morning. The night she saw it, a week or so later, we were at home doing nothing when the phone rang. It was about a quarter past eleven, and of course it was Patsy. "Put Frank on," she said evenly, when I answered the phone. I yelled to Frank and naturally stayed on the extension. "Really, Frank, it was awful," I heard her say. "I kept waiting for those great lines you quoted and they never came."

3) And here's how worked up he could get at the theater. He sat between Edwin Denby and me at *Long Day's Journey into Night*. Within minutes after the curtain went up, I could feel Frank bracing himself for the anguish that lay ahead; a little later, he noticed Edwin stirring uneasily in his seat. "Do you want to leave?" he whispered, actually reaching for his coat. Edwin said, "If you can stand it, I can." Then there was *Happy Days*. The first performance we saw, an afternoon run-through at the Cherry Lane, reduced us to tears. Emerging from the theater, still shaken from the experience, we ran into several people (Edward Albee and Ned Rorem among them) who, while impressed, seemed to Frank somewhat cautious in their praise. "Joe, let's get away from these awful people," he said more for their benefit than mine.

Some of these plays are so personal, or private, what with references to friends and in-jokes about them, that I wonder how they seem to readers who never moved in Frank's circle. One of them—the completely daffy *Coronation Murder Mystery*, an O'Hara-Ashbery-Koch collaboration written on the occasion of Jimmy Schuyler's thirty-third birthday and performed at a party in his honor—might remind the reader of nothing so much as children at play, dressing up in grown-ups' clothes and putting on a show in the backyard. But *Kenneth Koch, a Tragedy*, which Frank wrote with Larry Rivers, is another matter altogether. Bitchy and gossipy, it audaciously evokes some of the atmosphere of the downtown art-poetry scene of the fifties. Here we find such real-life characters as Jackson Pollock, drunk and abusive at the Cedar Bar ("Those fags," he says in reference to Frank and Larry); John Myers, already making claims for his importance as a force in the world of art and poetry ("I have a gallery of the liveliest, most original, and above all youngest, painters in America, and for every painter there's a poet"); Elaine de Kooning, advising Bill about selling his paintings in her inimitable brand of New Yorkese ("Nah don't cum dahn on yuh price, Bill . . ."); de Kooning himself, chatting and reminiscing in *his* inimitable style ("Yah, travel is okay, Poland, the marshes, it's terrific. It's like the signs I used to paint in Holland when I was a kit"); and above all, Kenneth Koch being kidded about, among other things, what Frank teasingly called his "H.D.," or homosexual dread, which in reality must have been Kenneth's understandable dismay at realizing that so many of his friends were gay ("They called me 'queer' and I thought they meant I was a poet, so I became a poet. What if I'd understood them? Moses! what a risk I was running"). If you weren't around then, this irreverent play will give you some idea what you missed. It was a scene, boozy and anything but cool, that quickly changed with the advent of rock, dope and pop art in the sixties, and the arrival of success (the heavy drinking, fighting and emotionalism of the Abstract Expressionist milieu were mostly due, I'm convinced, to lack of recognition).

My curiosity got the better of me, so I wrote and asked Bill Berkson about *Flight 115, or Pas de Fumer sur la Piste*. Here's what he wrote back, from Bolinas, Calif.:

Frank and I composed this little drama in November 1961 on a jet flight over the Atlantic returning to New York from Paris. Or from Rome via Paris, actually. We had spent two weeks in Paris, staying at Paul Jenkins' studio on Rue Vercingétorix and seeing a lot of John Ashbery (as well as the galley proofs of his book *The Tennis Court Oath*) and Joan Mitchell (who supplied us with the epigraph for *Flight*) and Jean-Paul Riopelle (who held forth beautifully one night at the Closerie des Lilas about Picabia). Then Rome, with witty and generous Bill Weaver as our guide to people and paintings, and a quickie tour (no Elizabeth Taylor in the bargain, alas!) of the Forum set for *Cleopatra* at Cinecittá, and a long pause in the Accatolico Cemetary with Keats and Shelley . . . The play's title is the PanAm flight number plus "No Smoking During Landing or Take-off." We has a conveniently small portable Hermes Rocket, which we passed back and forth, supporting it on our knees. Me in the window seat, Frank in the middle, and a man who described himself as "in government work" in the third (aisle) seat. Much of the play obviously attempts to fathom the inner-monolog process of this mystery-companion who could not conceal his perplexity (suspicion?) at us enjoying the novelty of the collaboration-at-30,000-feet. Every so often this third-who-flew-beside-us would lean over his armrest to demand, "Are you sure you really are Americans???" Maybe that was because so many of the lines in this play pretend to be in foreign languages. Or maybe they got that way because he asked?

In the mid-sixties I used to run into Andy Warhol at some of Kenward Elmslie's parties on Cornelia Street. At the time, Andy was making short movies that had nothing going on in them except people kissing, eating bananas, getting a blow job, etc., etc. One night I drunkenly suggested that for a change he make a long movie with lots of plot. He seemed intrigued, so I dreamed up the idea of asking all the poets and writers I knew to contribute episodes; I would supply the continuity, and the movie would be called *Messy Lives,* a title Bill Berkson gave me. I mentioned all of this to Frank. Before I decided what the movie's frame would be, he wrote an episode called *Love on the Hoof* with Frank Lima. Then Edwin Denby wrote something, and so did Ron Padgett. And that's as far as the project got; I'm not even sure Andy was ever really interested in the idea, though he did go on to make his first long movie, *Chelsea Girls,* a year or so later. Edwin's episode has disappeared and Ron's is stuck away somewhere, he tells me. But what the two Franks wrote has found its way into this volume.

Steve Rivers, Larry's son, was Frank's youngest collaborator; he couldn't have been more than seven or eight when he wrote *Shopping for Joe* with Frank. The "Joe" they were shopping for was Joe Rivers, and I guess it was his birthday. On other occasions, when Frank visited Larry in Southampton, he collaborated with Steve on poems. Like so many works of Frank's they apparently haven't survived—though I've heard that some of the poems, copies of which Steve doesn't have, are among Frank's papers.

That brings up the question: How many plays of Frank's were lost, anyway? Two I've known about for sometime: he never saw *The Thirties* again after checking it along with other things in a Penn Station locker and then losing the key, and *The Houses at Falling Hanging* was last seen after he'd given it to somebody at the Living Theater. Frank also worked with me on a play and a couple of TV scripts whose whereabouts I've lost track of. And now, in his letter to James Broughton, I read about another play not included in this collection. (Frank, by the way, was writing to Broughton in response to a request for plays by Frank and other New York poets for possible production in San Francisco). He writes: "Another play of my own I would like you to see is *The Moon Also Rises;* unlike the other two it is about some contemporaries on a weekend in the suburbs and is rather funny (in verse). I think it would play but but I can't find it. A young actress named Irma Hurley had it last I think and then went to the coast for Tennessee's *Garden District.* Perhaps you have met her and could ask her if she knows anything about it . . ." As you can see, Frank had a terrible habit of not making copies of things he wrote; this was mainly because he could get what he wanted in one draft. But who knows? Maybe one of these plays—and more poems—will surface sometime in the future.

Joe LeSueur
New York, March, 1978

[PROLOGUE]

Pagliaccio   Orazio
Harlequin   Cinthio
Pierrot   Doctor Baloardo
Columbine   Brighella
Isabella   Fenocchio
Captain   Pantaloon
Pulcinella   Scaramouche

PAGLIACCIO:
Good evening, ladies and gentlemen! Welcome
to Italy! It was audacious of our troupe, was
it not? to meet you here at the airfield just
descended from your plane, before you have even
gone to the toilet? we shall have to be very
good performers to amuse under such circumstances!
But that is what we like! We all perform much
better under adverse circumstances such as these,
hah! I mean circumstances that affect our
audience adversely, for we could not be expected
to act well if we ourselves were other than,
how is it said? in the prime? But to proceed:
airfield! what a delightful term! field of air!
There it is above you, from that great column
you have just descended, slid down, as it were,
haha! into our pleasant land. Airfield. Yet do
not think that the heavens are any more fabulous
than the contrivances of emotion and improvisation
you are about to witness. No! we are as fleet and
as beautiful as the birds in this, our own sky!
And lest you, with your American ideas of skill

1

and organization, grow restless during our Skit, let me remind you that there is no gratuitous act. Watch carefully, that the design, subtle and as pervasive as the circulation of the blood, and as thorough, may be revealed to you. Let this first gesture since your departure from your native land be one of the imagination. Invite us, by the quickened tempo of your heartbeats, to strike three times upon our primitive tambour and with the speed of true magic acts raise the curtain from your hearts. Yes? YES!

Pagliaccio runs clumsily off stage in his floppy costume and after the third quick but distinct beat the curtain sweeps up! The stage is empty! that is, it is partially ready for a performance, but there are not actors on it, and some properties seem to be missing. There is a great deal of chatter from backstage, but no more than the number of characters who eventually appear would warrant. And they do appear hurriedly, carrying with them a few more pieces of stage furniture or property, scurrying about to put these in the right place. Then they take places and face the audience somewhat embarrassedly. One mutters quite loudly "Oh dear!", and after some nudging, one of the other, someone at last says something. "Harlequin!"

Act 1

Harlequin steps forward, makes an elegant leg to the audience, then turns to the other players. "Well!" he shouts. In profile to the audience he throws out his arms, jumps into the air, and lands with a bounce, screeching "SCRAM!" They all mill around, trying to decide on an unimpeded exit. At this Harlequin turns to the audience and shrugs. Then he looks at the players, leaps again shouting "PIERROT!" Pierrot turns from the others and comes down stage to Harlequin. The other players disappear.

HARLEQUIN:
Well where were you
going! Who is servant
to whom around here!
Is it my job to
remind you of every
little thing you
ought to do? For god's
sake, Pierrot. . . .

PIERROT:
But sir!
There's a mistake!

HARLEQUIN:
Oh! oh! I beg your
pardon! my friend
Pierrot, for god's
sake, how ridiculous!
I am a fool. Forgive
me. Where is that
damned Scaramouche!

The fault is mine dear   *(to the audience)*
sirs. Pierrot is not
my servant but my fond
friend. I suppose that's
why I called on him in
the confusion. Really
it's no easy thing to
improvise. It's like
crossing a busy street!

Ah Pierrot, my dear. You
will forgive me, won't
you? Have I embarrassed
you? But where is Scara-
mouche, thàt louse! that . . .

PIERROT:
Here he comes now,
Harlequin. There are
lots of other people
with him: Columbine
and the Captain and
ah! the beautiful,
the glorious, the

HARLEQUIN:
slovenly

PIERROT:
Franceschina!
Harlequin! I'll not
have you say those
things about her! You
do not know her!

HARLEQUIN:
No,
but it is only my
good taste which has
prevented me.
But
quick, Pierrot, be
kind! forgive me! I
cannot stay, but do
please send Scaramouche
to me at once. I can
not bear to see all
these old faces so
early in the morning.
Remember! Adieu!

(runs off stage as others enter from opposite side, chatting and preening, dancing a bit, merry, except for Columbine, who is in tears.)

4

COLUMBINE:
(Isabella is talking and flirting with Captain)
Oh mistress! Mistress! oh!
Oh! oh! oh! oh! Mistress I-
sabella!

ISABELLA:
What is wrong with you?

COLUMBINE:
I am wronged in-
deed. Oh mistress be kind!
Find out Harlequin and hang
him! He is a beast a worm a
pig and a bastard! If you knew!
you would burst with outrage!
I shall tell you. He came to me
with honeyed words, such
honey! and won me to him for
the forty hundredth time!
It was terrible. You know how
pretty he is. He danced he
played with me he sang me
songs of devotion and quite
unseemly adoration which denied the gods and won me
completely. He threatened to
go mad, to die, to fall in a
fit! What could I do? he blushed
fainted swore and finally
kissed me. The moon was up.
The sky was sparkling with
stars. Could anything untoward
happen on such a well-lit
night? How could I have guessed
what wild thoughts were burning
into mine from his daring
eyes? You know how I have

always longed to live in a
diamond! His eyes sparkled
darkly like the fire in a
bedroom, his lips drew out
with ardor and pain like a
wizard's rhombus, and his chest
fairly moaned against my . . .
dress. I thrust him away
into a juniper bush but he
sprang back gracefully. His
thighs in those diamond
tights! Mistress! I was his
before I could say Yes!

The company sighs sympathetically and Franceschina comes for-
ward to put an arm about Columbine, swaying to and fro with her
in her passion.

And now he has gone! Left
me alone. What shall I do?
How can I live?. . . .

The company nods sagely and sighs some more; Franceschina is
sobbing freely when Columbine suddenly throws her off, bounces to
the center of the stage, and with legs spread bellows to the others:

AND BEAR HIS BRAT! BAH!

Then Columbine breaks into tender and affecting tears, runs to
her mistress and falls at her hem sobbing:

Oh mistress Isabella for-
give me! I beg you, my
wretched condition brings
me to this rudeness, You will
forgive and be kind, oh
mistress, won't you? I am
too young for this, too
pretty, too clever. I was

6

swept away by the tricky
little . . . dancer! Oh mistress
my waist will grow big, my
teeth will fall out, my
breasts will hang to the
ground and all because of
him! Oh Harlequin, oh love!

CAPITANO:
Ah, Lady Isabella, your pretty maid suffers.
Permit me to avenge her for your sweet sake.
The man must be a thorough scoundrel to allow
such a lovely one to languish after gaining
his indubitable pleasure. For your own sake
and the sake of your sweet ladies in waiting
grant me the charge of seeking out this cock,
this showy feathered flatterer, and beating
him hastily with the flat of my cavalry saber!
Grant me this boon and your handkerchief as
token in the discharge of this sweet duty!
Let me prove to you that there are men of honor
and moral graciousness near to your loveliness
who would go forth to the death to defend a
lady's honor. Ahem! or a maid's!

PULCINELLA:
                    Oh mercy! oh
gracious! oh balls! the poor little spindly
Harlequin will kill you surely Captain. Oh
dear me yes! quite dead dead dead and clumsy
for the sake of your sweet pretty lady love
who will then be free to distribute her well-
and-popularly-computed fleshly largesse to
the amorous and handsomer-than you-are young
Cinthio del Sole or the gallant legged Orazio!
Haw! Christ yes, Captain, you'll have the best
of her, her handkerchief can neither withdraw
at the ultimate moment nor cheat you afterwards,
nor, unless it be very very soiled (the more

7

fool you) get you into unseemly medical ex-
penses! Haw! haw! haw! poor Harlequin at the
hands of this monster. Run Scaramouche and tell
your master to run ahead of you from this fierce
lion, this bull of the infantry, this eagle of
the stockyard! this self-report from the battle
front of [e]very way since Adam! haw! haw! haw!

*Pulcinella ogles fiercely and stamps his foot at the Captain, racing
behind Brighella and Doctor Baloardo as the Captain charges
slapping at him with drawn sword. Isabella is in a state of extreme
vexation. The two gallants, Orazio and Cinthio del Sole are much
amused and shout in mock consternation after the Captain.*

ORAZIO & CINTHIO:
(unison)
Captain! Captain! he wrongs us
we are innocent of such a vile
intent: to wrong to wrong the
innocentest love in all the
land the love you bear fair
Isabella. The loveliest love
in all the land, the most ad-
mirable, we admit it the un-
surpassably proud and fierce
love you bear the lady in your
heart . . . . .

*Unnoticed by the Captain, who is entangled with Doctor Baloar-
do, Pierrot, Brighella and his brother Fenocchio, Pantaloon, and
Scaramouche, the two cease from lack of breath, and ogle the ladies
proudly and humorously. Pulcinella has meanwhile escaped into
the wings. The Captain blindly grabs Pierrot and shakes his valet
fiercely hanging onto him as if he were trying to escape, which he
certainly is not. The ladies scream with laughter.*

CAPTAIN:
There! villain, slanderer and foul-tongued dog!
8

Hunchbacked wartnosed troublemaker. Cowardly
slanderer! oh! oh! roustabout bastard! chicken-
tongued malefactor! villain slanderer and foul-
tongued dog! Oh! oh! oh! etc.

PIERROT:
It is not I, it cannot be
that you mean me! oh take
not these tears for guilt!
If these accusations are
meant in sincerity then
shake me till you're sure
my innocence is proven by
my meek endurance or if not
then from death's serenity
my innocence and loyal love
will shine forth as from a
glassy mask which cannot
change intentions to defeat
its meaning as the human
face only too often and too
unreasonably does. Oh Captain
remember the love you bear
your loyal servant, Captain!

*The Captain comes to his senses and seats himself on a block in the
middle of the stage with Pierrot on his lap. In consternation he lets
go of Pierrot, who falls to the floor, sitting up-right at the Captain's feet and slightly to his side, while the Captain punches a
knee with his elbow and slams his chin on his fist in perplexity.
Then he looks at Pierrot sitting terrified and large-eyed before
him. They both forget the other players, who stand at the back
acutely interested in the scene.*

CAPTAIN:
Pierrot, was it you? I
grabbed you and beat you
unmercifully! you? my
own servant Pierrot?

9

PIERROT:
Yes, Captain. I kept
shouting in mortal
terror of my life, yet
knowing you had the
right to demand it; I
being your servant.

CAPTAIN:
No Pierrot. I have not
any such right. No, no.
*(He pats Pierrot's chin and Pierrot smiles ravishingly and wiggles
his knees.)*
That I should mistake
you for Pulcinella, that
foul-nosed wretch, is
what hurts me, my pretty
Pierrot. No, no, what
should I do without you
if you were offended and
left me? I should have
to act the braggart with
everyone then, have no
rest and no intimacy! A
dreadful prospect! I
should soon go mad and
murmur "Pierrot Pierrot
has gone whither?" all
over Italy searching. And
most likely never find
you. I never can find anything without your help.
Am I forgiven by my only
friend, my own fragile
Pierrot?

PIERROT:
        Master, I could
not other than forgive you.

I seem myself brave and big
in your bold eyes, no longer
fragile. You have only in a
fit of temper struck your
head against a wall and
now, the anger being over,
we are both made well.

CAPTAIN:
                    My
sweet loyal Pierrot. You
are right. We shall know
ourselves next time, eh?

*The crowd behind them suddenly breaks into loud and embarrass-
ing cat calls and shouts, such as "A pretty scene!" "Oh my yes!"
"Bis! bis!" "Oh Captain!" "O Pierrot!" Scaramouche darts arro-
gantly forward, strutting, and taps Pierrot patronisingly on the tip
of his hat, squashing it.*

SCARAMOUCHE:
Oh Pierrot, I thought I
was your best friend. Oh
now I am hurt. My heart
is broken! Hah! And you
dear sir! I guess neither
the ladies, NOR Harlequin
need worry about your
sword NOR . . . .

*The Captain draws and chases Scaramouche off stage with bellows
of rage while Pierrot sits pathetically stage front dabbing at his
eyes.*

[Ann Arbor, 2/51]

[Editors' note: Manuscript breaks off here.]

11

[PRELUDE]

Gordon
Marianne
Jack

Neil
Chorus of Villagers
Dotty

GORDON:
At this the two boys parted in order to pursue their similar
pursuits, the one blond, the other . . . . . blond. As you can
readily imagine the sun had risen on a day quite other, too.
The earth was in a state of extreme nervous warmth, the people somewhat relieved by humidity and airplanes, those
crashing bores. At the sight of Mother Eglantine our two
heroes (she was placed very high as it were!) bumped into
each other for the space of two blocks muttering the syllables
"Words!" and "Evoi!" under each other's breath; then dashed
off in opposite lacks of directions once more.

MARIANNE:
Oh my darling twins, my almost twins, my boys! May God
protect them on this, their initial departure which always
threatens to be final. It's what the word "initial" means. And
why were they muttering those particular words? If only
you'd overheard them saying something more reassuring to
each other like "baseball" or "money"; then we'd know that
they'd stick together through thick and thin, help each other
out in all sorts of difficulties, identify and respond—and return finally safe to harbor. My darlings!
    Oh I'm sorry, my dear, to carry on. You must be as worried
as I am. Surely Mother Eglantine, in her dark robes, will be
able to spy on them in the city. Nuns can get away with anything because they're always really thinking of something
else.

13

Some people wander on as if the stage were a street. It becomes darker, but they are not particularly sinister in appearance, the men in shirtsleeves, the women in cotton dresses, both somewhat mussed and unkempt.

GORDON:
The boys are at just the age to demand freedom and independence. It will pass, they will return to us for food. Let them wander for a day or two in the city which is not far off, it seems like a palace to them.
(Sudden rage)
When they come back I'll break the both of them I swear to God I will!

Marianne screams and turns away. Gordon turns towards her, and both see the boys suddenly appear in the middle of the group of people, walking.

JACK:
Not the intrusion of the multitude, but a feeling of hardness at the core of the heart, a tingling amorousness which only large numbers of people arouse.

NEIL:
Yes, and the knowledge that distance is only the pressure of one body upon another, locked in a sweaty embrace which is at the ultimate moment resented and withdrawn from at so rapid a pace that the sound of locomotives careening upon hidden tracks in a mountain echoes always at dusk against the flesh that had so willingly become a wall. So willingly turned from the glowing eager face to the cold sea and thought of solitude as a stimulus to virtue, little guessing how finally the word "No" blasts its image into the overhanging summit of the heart, visible to motorers . . . . Hey! let's get out of here.

They have disappeared into the crowd and thence into the wings as Marianne and Gordon move towards them, shocked at seeing them, yet not having comprehended what they said.

14

Act 1

CHORUS OF VILLAGERS:
Welcome to our daylit village
deep up in the fleecy sea,
where witches don't wait for Sabbath
and wandering's what's not we.

At evening and at morning
we wing and carol freely,
warning our Dotty of intrigue,
love and poison, amorously, wittily.

She with her flaxen heartstrings
has wound around the mountains
roving the slopes with amber cartwheels
she turns our shoulderblades to fountains.
        (They weep.)

DOTTY:
Ah! Aaaaaaaaaaaaah! Goody! The dazzling light of morning
does push-ups on every blade of grass, tender frolicsome kiss-
ers! And the darling heart of a maiden famous in her own no-
torious village, screams with the darling ambition of what
when she is thirty-five will be contemptuously described by
the simple-minded townies and gossiping fairies as PASsion.

[Editors' note: Manuscript breaks off here.]

TRY! TRY!,
a Noh play

Notes on the Noh Play relevant to TRY! TRY!:
The Noh plays are ancient ritual one-act plays of Japan. The audience once dressed for them as if for a religious service in elaborate ceremonial robes. The interest is in suggested action or tensions, and in the lyrics, dances and formalized gestures. The decor is symbolical. The musicians—traditionally three drums, and a flute—appeared on stage. The actors stamped their feet at the conclusion of their speeches. The movement is photographic rather than dramatic. The audience is supposed to know all the plays by heart.

Presented by the Poets' Theatre, Cambridge, Massachusetts, February 26, 1951. Directed by V.R. Lang, with lighting by Nancy Ryan and Charles E. Eisitt, sets and costumes by Edward St. John Gorey and Alison Bishop, with Hugh Amory as stage manager and the following cast:

VIOLET	V. R. Lang
JOHN, a friend of the Poet's	John Ashbery
JACK, Violet's husband	Jack Rogers

Scene: A kitchen. There is a window rear center above the sink, but no furnishings other than an ironing board and a small table with an old-fashioned gramophone on it. As the scene opens Violet is leaning on the ironing board and John is playing a recording of a slow waltz.

17

Time: *After any war.*

Persons: VIOLET *and* JACK, *husband and wife reunited after the war; and* JOHN, *a friend of the poet.* VIOLET *is dressed in a shabby, prewar pink party dress,* JOHN *in a dark suit,* JACK *in uniform.* JOHN *should stop the gramophone for his own speeches but sometimes play appropriate music during the others'. The gestures should be extremely stylized throughout, and the lighting should help to emphasize this formality, perhaps, for instance, by a center light over the ironing board into the ring of which the characters would have to step to be seen during their speeches. It might be nice to have* JOHN *follow the other two characters' lines with a copy of the script, dropping the pages ostentatiously to the floor as the play went on, one by one.*

VIOLET:
(alone)
My name is Violet. It's not
a pretty name. It's not a name
that any beauty ever had. I,
hearing it called through bars
or playgrounds or hospitals,
am not reminded of the flower.
I avoid my name whenever I can,
as a matter of fact, with any
other name. Oh dear, I'm sick
of the color and the smell that
ever since childhood everyone's
taken great delight in rubbing
in. Even the most ridiculous di-
minutives are pleasanter to
my ears. But if only he'd return
what blessed boredom it would be
to hear my name pronounced with
the right degree of propriety.

*(*JOHN *has been standing in a listening attitude, half in and half out of the light. He removes the record from the phonograph and steps towards* VIOLET.*)*

18

JOHN:
I'm afraid the girl will not be
entirely satisfactory. When the poet
talked with me the Violet we knew
was not like this. Her wit seems
to have been dried or dulled. We look
for abundance of feeling, to counteract
the sterility of war. She is a woman
after all. My girl, you cannot simply
stand and wait. When he comes home
your Jack will have enough to bear
without this black fatigue you
seem to be in all the time.

VIOLET:
I know. Perhaps if I thought deliberately
of time before the war?

JOHN:
                    Yes, that might help.

VIOLET:
Then everything seemed younger somehow
and the world dressed up too much.

I always favored a party dress, always
in those days, with net stockings, and a bright

bangle in my slick straight hair. I never
used to lie, either. I was a real joke among

my friends for being so anxiously stupid
about the truth. Life went by so fast then!

There was a great deal of laughter, and you didn't
dare to lie because the next moment was

upon you! with a fast and confounding surprise.
That's why I had so many dresses: everything

19

was a special event, and the most unusual
found me eager and waiting. Oh, I used to

go through all my dresses every night before
dinner, so that Jack could hardly tell whether

dish or Violet were the greater surprise. I used to
sing annoyingly in his ear all the time.

Because I invariably felt stark naked.

JOHN:
My dear!
I hadn't meant you to go on so. Please
don't feel bad.

VIOLET:
That's all right. I don't know
how I feel. Except that I'm never naked

any more. You know how it is when the music's
over? I spent the war dancing. I'm just tired.

JOHN:
Oh Violet, at no time has the poet
or myself touched or questioned your
generosity or need. How could I
have presumed to criticize you?
I remember you in the bars and the
cafes with your dirty face and
shabby hose, smiling and singing
so cleverly, just as if you were happy.
And I know you didn't always get
the biggest sailor in the fleet.

VIOLET:
Don't go on. It's not fun
to be understood when you didn't know
you had to be. How

else could I make myself feel real
in that dazzled time?
I only tried to be felicitous.
When the lights are up
I've got to shout and kick or go blind.
I'm afraid I'm the sort
of girl that sings in the movies, along
with the heroine. Or
disappears altogether until intermission.

JOHN:
It's not easy to be
spectator or audience.
Always overruled by
someone else's plan
of what you really want.
Violet, you're never asked
what news you want to see
in the paper. When will
he, Jack, come home?

VIOLET:
As if waiting for someone besides me
to ask that question had delayed him,
now he appears, limping up the walk.

And after all these years of sorting
my feelings and piling them about
the kitchen, ready, classified and

clean, I don't know what I feel. I
wish I had more time to decide. Oh
why did I say that? I'm crying.

JOHN:
Jack created this emptiness
by his departure. You cannot, fill,
        Violet, the cupboard
        where the colander

21

hung dry, the plane
of linoleum a stove
once stabilized,
the empty shelves
and racks for cloths
and pots and dishes,
the windows void
even of a view
not with the most appropriate sentiments.
Does Jack know what he had done here?

VIOLET:
Oh I don't know I
don't know! Be still.

(But they cease their agitation when JACK *appears.* JACK *and* VIO-
LET *freeze into odd wooden positions staring at each other. The
lighting increases.* JOHN *moves with a tentative dignity to a position between* VIOLET *and* JACK.*)*

JOHN:
In this moment of silence the expected
lyricism begins. As when the subway stops
just before reaching a station, they breathe heavily
for a minute, all of a minute, though very sure
of the time, his hand on her lips; her eyes
stirring. They allow the world this minute to speak
before taking up their love again, and softly
as a gift the world tells them what images they make,
how it spies upon them every night, what
their death will be, and how magical they are.

VIOLET:
Oh Jack! my Jackson!
why did you leave me?
Since you left I've had
to sell the flute and the
bath-tub. And my voice
is broken. I'll never

again sing you "Trail
of the Lonesome Pines."
And Jackson, I'm glad
you're back. Just don't
look at my fingernails.

(The light dims again. VIOLET *slumps over the ironing board,
holding her arms out stiffly in front, and* JACK *ceremoniously removes his cap and jacket and hangs them over her clasped hands.*
JOHN *has moved back to the gramophone and has put on a rather
dissonant record.* JACK *moves stage front for his speech and only
the last two lines of it are addressed to* VIOLET *specifically as he
turns from the audience to her.)*

JACK:
I've come a long way for your sake,
my back all decorated like this
and my feet covered with mold. Do
you know why they had to put fire
under my lids?
            When we first went
riding, how like dashing Cossacks!
it was easy then to dress in scarlet.
I sat my mount prettily and hacked
babies and old women with a song
on my breath—I even let my eyebrows
grow! and with the gold braid and all
I frightened myself.
            There were sweet
times, and we weren't too drunk to
appreciate them. Lovely ladies loved
us, like useful flowers. And as I say,
my color was good. I had a beautiful
horse.
            Why, I thought of myself as
Eric's son, Lief, going towards
the moon with a world behind me
and a lot of blood to get off my
chest. I wanted to bellow the green

and black waves flat and then
cleave my way like an iceberg! I was
good, and I knew it. I hadn't laid
them all low for nothing: women
and villages, coasts of islands
twice as big as Iceland. And didn't
they all squat when I frowned, even
my bad old father? But something
went wrong. One minute I was lord of
all I surveyed, and the next I knew
that I'd be beaten—that I'd better
go back to my easy throne, and leave
this virgin land I'd first laid
heavy hands upon. That was a
retreat! how I cried to shove off
from that rich tough land, my
kind of country, and go home!
What was it that beat me? the
land, the air, the sun, all
bigger than the gods intended
me to own? I yearned after it,
and it grew like a spiral as I
thought through the years of
my Vinland the Good.
                         Or I was the
Admiral, bossing a bothersome
crew and pretending a good deal
of confidence, when suddenly there
was a hint of glory! I didn't
believe it, just because the
seaweed looked like fresh grass;
I knew I might be feverish and I
didn't plan to be taken in, but
there was something in the air—
a sweetness like finding a ruby
when you were looking for a baseball—
and at the same time I was scared
at not knowing, it was mine and I
hadn't planned for it, I wasn't

strong enough, and anyone could
knock me down, all those others
who wanted everything as much as
I did.

   So I spent most of my time
wondering when bullets, mortars and
bombs were going to find out where
my courage ended and this cowardice—
oh intuition, I'm not on trial, am I?—
began. Finally a sniper in a tree
on the edge of the Pacific's
exciting waters—an oriental with
lots of time for meditation—
saw me clearly. At the right moment.
It was time, you see, not
topographical, like Achilles' heel.
I was thinking of myself as heir
to the Mississippi. My thoughts moved
to De Soto—whose wouldn't? And
that was when I was spotted, naked
as the beach, caught within a few feet
of safety. Have you ever thought
about men like him,—who could
have been emperors? I fell like a
sail, relaxed, with no surprise.
Had the war started for me to kill
or be killed? I don't know. I did
feel that something had been completed.
You think you know what that means?
Perhaps you do! I think I do!

   *(The lights have come up slowly during the last of the speech. At
   JACK's last words VIOLET straightens up seriously, dropping his
   clothes to the floor, and JOHN yanks the gramophone silent.)*

   JOHN:
For god's sake, Jack! this
is no way to talk! she's had
her own visitors. Trying to

drive the blues away. Ladies
compulsive and never friendly,
willing Violet nothing but
their shoes. Your wife, after all!

(VIOLET *withdraws to center rear in a light against the window.*
JOHN *turns back to his machine and puts on a melancholy record.*)

VIOLET:
Children wade on the receding shingle
gaunt in their practiced grace. Mature,
they ape their elders and cavort like
pogo sticks in the advancing foam.

Where well-mannered aeroplanes and autos
serenely sail, on the yellow sand, children
ignore their own innocence. They've taken it all
in, and know how they want their backs broken.

(JOHN *stops the music and looks at* VIOLET. *She seems not to hear*
JACK *when he speaks.*)

JACK:
So that's it. Well.
Why didn't you do something about it
while I was away?
Surely you weren't
just thinking of
my idea of Columbus.
To make sleep real.

VIOLET:
I would like to fill a jungle
with elephants and gorillas and
boa constrictors. I would like
to fill the trees and waterfalls
with the blackness in me, so I
might be a bird of paradise.

26

It would be fun to break a bottle
of wine and have it turn to
water. Or shoot a clay pigeon
and have it go honk! honk! and
lay an egg in the marshes. I'd
rather not be a wedding guest.

If I were the Sphinx I could lie
in the sun and stare at myself
with pure white eyes. When I smiled
airplanes would go off their courses.
I'd hold down the dark and
say sweet nothings to the palms.

(The lighting becomes again central and as VIOLET moves back
into the group JOHN leaves the gramophone.)

JOHN:
Oh that's what we'd all do
Violet! But we never have the
chance! Oh did the poet know
this would happen when he dragged
us into this? A friend of mine!

JACK:
Stop it! It's not the poet's
fault. I'm the one who went
away. Then I had Violet's love.
Always, at first, like a charm.
But you can't carry memory
everywhere. It's heavy. It hurts.
Violet, I left your love in
barracks and hotels as well
as battlefields. I'm sorry.

VIOLET:
Your anger beats out
even in your most reposed

moments: and my bitterness
varies every I love you.

We go together like a
hand-organ and monkey
or diadem and bull-head.
And fear each other's death.

Oh Jack! this is when married
people try to be beautiful!
it's not enough that you're back
if nothing is changed!

*(VIOLET and JACK take a step away from each other and freeze,
staring elsewhere. JOHN takes up his position between VIOLET and
JACK.)*

JOHN:
Now I remember how the poet feels about knowing,
that it is better, and in itself an end.

Violet, you'll keep on grubbing in the laundry
hoping for something lovely and disturbing

like a crystal hand emerging with a sparkler.
And Jack, you'll make her weep because you

both are too familiar, and she's already used to
dancing in the dark while you're asleep

or not around; and your heroes really are all dead.
We all know that this goes on and on and on.

But Violet, remember how moved we've been,
and forget that the kitchen's full of knives.

(CURTAIN)

28

AN EPILOGUE: to the Players of *Try! Try!*

1 John Ashbery

If I get sick you'll fly
to me, John, and not eat dinner
on the plane for sheer worry.

If it's night the red lights
will affright you of my blood letting,
and your verse will flood

with memories of all those
choral compositions on prison themes
we both have so enjoyed.

Indeed, my health will fail
in apprehension for your nerves, then
rally to greet you strongly.

The words I write for your voice
will always, I hope, resound as your own
lilting and agate love of ears.

2 Jack Rogers

Not lissome and not
gruntingly wholesome, your

humor's a Rasputin of emphasis,
Jack, a charade in front of

Mother Superior, the sub-
stantial unwillingness to

charm that frightens our
giggles into eager screeches!

Your grin across a room
makes me draw a sabre to

charge my nearest and
dearest friend for the fun

of it! And your voice in
my typewriter attempts to

tease the wit out of serious
situations, so we won't be

wrong goosing psychiatrists
for the sake of our guts.

                              3 Violet Lang
Image of all felinities
and Grand Lady of the
turnpikes, in decadent verse
you'd be a giantess but I,
in good health, exclaim you
mine! and speak familiarly.

Dancer always, to me, and
tea room's despaired-of *voyou*,
you are my Bunny and other
people's Violet, a saint of
circumstance and the dangerous
Birthday Party. I quote you
back to yourself in all women
and love you as if *Symposium*
had not been writ in jest.

Kiss me. We'll never again fight
in a cafeteria of friends. I want
your voice in my ear so the sun
will be hotter, and as Bermudas
make us dizzy we'll clamber over
mountains as red and yellow as
clowns, shouting to John and Jack:
"hurry up! Poo, poo! Tra la!"

30

TRY! TRY!

To Anne Meacham

[Note: This is the second play of this title and with these characters. The present play is not a second version, but an almost completely new play written for the New York cast and for the decor of Larry Rivers.]

Presented by the Artists' Theatre, New York City, February 1953. Directed by Herbert Machiz, with a setting designed by Larry Rivers, music by John LaTouche, lighting by Mildred Jackson, and the following cast:

JOHN	Jack Cannon
VIOLET	Anne Meacham
JACK	Louis Edmonds

Place: *A studio.*

Scene: *A room. A war has ended. The two are sitting on an old wicker sofa, listening to a phonograph record.*

JOHN:
I like songs about hat-check girls,
elevators, bunions, syphilis, all the
old sentimental things. It's not enough
to be thoughtful, is it?

31

VIOLET:
Aren't you acting terribly prewar?

JOHN:
My dear, I want you to work hard at
reinstating that wifely melancholy that
made you such a distinctive asset to
anyone "marching off" as they say. You
used to mourn for him like a model house.
Now the neighbors are all saying you've
gone down the drain. All I can say is
what a drain! I prefer to think you were
always a little too nice. "If anyone
cries in the world. . . .

VIOLET:
. . . it has to be me." Please stop trying
to cheer me up. Jesus. You're as relaxing
as a pin. I was a sweet, eager, pretty, and
energetic girl. As he remembers me, so
shall he find me. What ever made me take you
on as an added complication! You fill the
house. Or maybe it's me. I do burn a little
cork every time the smell of apple blossoms
drifts in the window. I haven't been burning
any lately though.

JOHN:
I could move out. I could just move out.

VIOLET:
Oh no. I want you here for evidence that I've
gone bad. I think you'll do the trick. Do
you hear a radio in the distance?

JOHN:
Don't change the subject. Why don't you wash
a few clothes before he gets back? I think
cerise would be a nice color for eventide.

Shall we mop the skylight?

VIOLET:
What's the sense? With all these miserable
distances and the praying mantises the only
people who ever look in. It isn't as if we
had to fear snoops or try to please them.
It's our own little place, for the time being.

JOHN:
I'm afraid Jack will see us before we see him.
And then out I'd go like a cloud,
lonely for my temporarily own disgusted little
flower and playmate, the best on the beach .

VIOLET:
You like to think you're involved with me
emotionally but what you're involved with
really is my lack of suitable clothes to
make an impression on the narrow world of
your narrow forehead. Some girls would say
you're stupid, but I'm not that patriotic.
No, you really are very sweet. Or at least
you have been. On occasion.

JOHN:
That was V day and the flags were out.

VIOLET:
I know you love me. *(They kiss.)* I didn't
know you loved me so much. What a magnifi -
cent gesture. I feel like a tube of hot
cement. What a lover, it's just like the
old days when the crows were in the corn
field and the rain was in the sky. You do
make me happy.

JOHN:
But it upsets me that you're never happy

for long. You know, Vi, I had big plans for
us. I thought we'd start a pet shop, a
little world of our own full of fondling and
loyalty and all the tiny things we've missed,
like ripples on a brook.

VIOLET:
You haven't talked this way since that afternoon in Arlington Cemetery when the football
game was being broadcast over the car radio.
Come off it, you're no gangster of the sheets.
When I was little I promised myself not to
fall in love with anyone but the best polo
pony in the western world. Polo is a very
interesting sport, second only to duck fighting
in polls of national taste. What kind of lip-
stick did I have on?

JOHN:
Raspberry. Right?

VIOLET:
I knew you didn't love me.

JOHN:
You never knew. You don't know now. You'll
never be able to guess I don't and I'll
never give you any security on that score.
What do you want from life anyway? If you
weren't so elegant in all the intimate areas
where a man needs a lilting simplicity we
might have flamed like a rubber tire.

VIOLET:
You're cute as a pumpkin. I wonder what Jack
will look like. Do you think he'll still
love me? I hope so. If not, I may have been
premature in certain plans I've laid for your
so sustaining mouth.

JOHN:
You know it isn't very warm in here.

VIOLET:
I'd like to think about that remark but
inattention has become such a habit—
it's interesting and what you say is not.
Isn't that blue I see, poking its nose
over the picture frame falling down the
side of the moonlit mountain to the east
of the capitol? A screaming as of brakes.
I hope it's a train, I mean a boat, coming
in. Maybe Jack will swim down its gang-
plank into my absent arms like he used to
at parties. He was the living proof that
all women are members of the same sex.

JOHN:
So is everybody else.

VIOLET:
Well, I guess some
men are just more alive than others.

JOHN:
I didn't know you were so fond of this
male war bride. You never muttered his
name by mistake in my palpitating arms at
certain moments when the news of the world
was noisily grunting through its telescope.

VIOLET:
Not by mistake, I didn't. Like everyone
conceited, you are not without cause. You
are by popular consent the best lay within
these four walls, and that acclaim shall
never be denied you by tender me.

JOHN:
My own!

35

VIOLET:
Dearest of all forgotten ones! *(They kiss.)*

JOHN:
Just think! Twice in one day. Our infatuation
is rearriving. What trouble it will arrange
to stir up in the next ten minutes between two
oh-so-troubled-and-disenchanted hearts!

VIOLET:
Yes. Yes. The trouble I long for. The trouble
that keeps me, and shall continue to keep me,
from realizing what trouble is. Dear John.
(They embrace.)

JOHN:
Hey. What's this nasty piece of wood stuck
In your boobs?

VIOLET:
Uh oh.

JOHN:
Well?

VIOLET:
It's a letter, a letter from Jack.

JOHN:
Well what are you carrying it around for?
Haven't you read it yet?

VIOLET:
Uh! *(She slaps him.)*

JOHN:
How come you never showed me this?

VIOLET:
You were never married to him.

JOHN:
When I think of the two of us, frail in our
affections, stranded on this planet of incessant
communication like gophers in their sweet-nosed
paralysis, or more similar to lovers who are very,
very sunburned! I marvel that we ever found it
possible or desirable to raise our lazy heads
from opposite ends of a gray fountain's inter-
section with the regimented air in order to just
say "Are you having fun?" to the dear person for
whom we are preparing, with passionately efficient
distraction, the deepest hurt, the one we did the
sweetly sweaty and individual push-ups and cold
creamings for, through the years. Doesn't it make
you marvel at human ambition? Is that a tear?

VIOLET:
Not on your life, you silly ass.
You can read the letter, don't carry on. No,
maybe you better not. It *is* my favorite letter.

JOHN:
Because, like all
sentimental women past their real gift-to-the-
world days, you're in love with your husband.
   (She dives for him. He grabs and pinions her.)

JOHN:
You want to toss me for who'll beat up whom?

VIOLET:
Oh read the damned thing!
   *(She breaks away from him and goes to the sculpture. During the
   letter-reading she drapes herself on it as if it represented the absent
   Jack to her.)*

JOHN:
I don't know if I'm well dressed enough. Where did
I put that rhinestone lavallière I stole from the
fairy at the ballet opening? Sit down, you silly

slut. You're not grappling with a stranger. One bite out of you and Jack won't know you from an ancient Kabuki.

VIOLET:
My hero! You're right out of a Noh play, aren't you? Prince Jasmine Jock, himself.

JOHN:
Oh boy, this is great. *(Reads:)*

Don't ever expect me to forget that moment of brilliance when your blue eyes lit the train station like a camera shutter. Your smile was like pink crinoline going though a ringer. Seventeen trains seemed to arrive and to bruisingly depart before I caught my breath sufficiently to ask you for a match. And then your perfume hit me like Niagara Falls.

Asked you for a match? What a relationship! Did he darn your aprons, too? Get this. *(Reads:)*

The pressure of being away from you is sometimes more than even the scenery can bear, and it is alarmingly brazen in piling snow over leaves and dark trunks lying across roads where the push of centuries is like a cymbal crashing in the roots of your hair. But I keep on dreaming of you whether awake or asleep as they say in songs, an azure dream. When I wake up, and I wake up every time I think of you, my prick presses against my belly like a log of foreboding, and I'm afraid that I'll die before I feel that thing that you are that nobody else is to my body, like a trembling insight into myself and the world I can't have. A train just went by covered with icy fir trees. The sky is white. I cry at night sometimes with my prick tangled in the sheets—wishing it would go away and find you and leave me alone in my, in this lousy southern country where it's colder in the winter than it ever is in the cold

countries. But all I do is bitch and what I mean is
I love you.

He has a funny style, doesn't he ? It seems like a pose
but it must be that he isn't used to writing. He
wasn't a journalist or anything, was he? They're
sometimes very awkward. I see now; you were hiding
it from embarrassment!

VIOLET:
I know it's enough for you that you amuse yourself,
so I won't complain of my own feelings. I do think I
despise you, but not as much as you would wish, or
I would wish. It's impossible that I could have
lived in precisely this airy derangement for this time
if any irony of yours could touch me deeply. It's not
that I love Jack! I hate my life.

JOHN:
Princess Lonelyhearts.

VIOLET:
Well let's not stop camping. We haven't seen the last
of each other, not us, not Little-Dimity-Head-Felt and
Bouncing-Broad-Britches. There's a tear left in this
magnificent vista yet. Just don't rust the pipes,
darling, and don't bump yourself tripping over the
arbutus. It's that green stuff with the velvet smile
that whines.

JOHN:
Dear god, I think that iron gate I put up as a weather
vane is creaking. An angel must be arriving.
Who do you suppose it could be?

VIOLET:
Well, one thing we have in common: we're both
    (primping)
beautiful people.

JOHN:
Yes, like a couple of cesspools.

VIOLET:
One season you're tan, you're happy, you're lying
beside an ocean, the hedges are shrinking with an
opium specific,

JOHN:
the next you're losing weight, you're cold, you're
getting bald, the floors are sealed against the
grovelling handclasp you extend into the bedrooms,
underneath the mezzanine.

VIOLET:
And when lust tries to make itself tangible but ends
up as the plot of your favorite silent movie over rye
and water under a slippery overhead mist, you want
that stranger you always awaited to hurry up, the
one you told everybody was an old friend who'd be
along in a minute.

JOHN:
A merchandise man from Chicago?

VIOLET:
No,
maybe an opera star who's retired for love.

*(They retire offstage amorously . JACK enters and stands silently
looking around. VIOLET and JOHN re-enter with a certain post-
coitus detachment from each other. After a pause:)*

JOHN:
Are you going to introduce me to the gentleman?

VIOLET:
Oh Jack! My Jackson!
why did you leave me?
40

Since you left I've had
to sell the flute and the
bathtub. And my voice
just froze. I'll never again
sing the popular songs
you composed while you were
on. Don't look at my fingernails.

JACK:
I've come along way for your sake,
my back all decorated like this
and my feet covered with mold. Do
you know why they had to put fire
under my lids?

JOHN:
He *is* like his letters!

VIOLET:
Shut up.

JACK:
When we first went
riding, how like dashing Cossacks!
It was easy then to dress in scarlet.
I sat my mount prettily and hacked
babies and old women with a song
on my breast—I even let my eyebrows
grow! and with the gold braid and all
I frightened myself. There were sweet
times and we weren't too drunk to
appreciate them. Lovely ladies loved
us, like useful flowers. And as I say
my color was good. I had a beautiful horse.
Why, I thought of myself as
Eric's son, Lief, going towards
the moon with a world behind me
and a lot of blood to get off my
chest. I wanted to bellow the green

41

and black waves flat and then
cleave my way like an iceberg! I was
good and I knew it. I hadn't laid
them all low for nothing: women
and villages, coasts of islands
twice as big as Iceland. And didn't
they all squat when I frowned, even
my bad old father? But something
went wrong. One minute I was lord of
all I surveyed, and the next I knew
that I'd be beaten—that I'd better
go back to my easy throne, and leave
this virgin land I'd first laid
heavy hands upon. That was a
retreat! how I cried to shove off
from that rich tough land, my
kind of country! and go home.
What was it that beat me? The land,
the air, the sun, all bigger than the
gods intended me to own? I yearned after it,
and it grew like a spiral as I thought
through the years of my Vinland the Good.
     (VIOLET *claps her hand over* JOHN'S *mouth.*)
Or if I was the
Admiral, bossing a bothersome crew
and pretending a good deal of confidence,
when suddenly there was a hint of glory!
I didn't believe it, just because the
seaweed looked like fresh grass; I knew
I might be feverish and I didn't want to
be taken in, but there was something in the
air—a sweetness like finding a ruby when
you were looking for a baseball—and at
the same time I was scared at not knowing,
it was mine and I hadn't planned for it,
I wasn't strong enough, and anyone could
knock me down, all those others who wanted
everything as much as I did.

JOHN:
Do I wake or sleep?

VIOLET:
I don't know.
I'm beginning to think I'm the one who's
been away all along. And still am.

JACK:
So I spent most of my time
wondering when bullets, mortars, and
bombs were going to find out where
my courage ended and this cowardice—
oh intuition, I'm not on trial am I?—
began. Finally a sniper in a tree
on the edge of the Pacific's
exciting waters—an oriental with
lots of time for meditation—
saw me clearly. At the right moment.
It was time, you see, not
topographical like Achilles' heel.
I was thinking of myself as heir
to the Mississippi. My thoughts moved
to De Soto—whose wouldn't? And
that was when I was spotted, naked
as the beach, caught within a few feet
of safety. Have you ever thought
about men like him—who could
have been emperors? I fell like a
sail, relaxed, with no surprise.
And here I am.

VIOLET:
By default, you mean.

JOHN:
Pardon me, I've got to take a terrific shit.

43

VIOLET:
You may as well put your pants on
before you come back.
    (JOHN *goes rear and dresses.*)

JACK:
Oh Violet!

VIOLET:
Now don't say anything you don't mean.
Just go on with the news bulletin. We're all
terribly interested in the outside world here.

JACK:
Well, if that's the way you feel. Who is
that anyway?

VIOLET:
A jazz musician named Lenny.

JACK:
He's billed as John under the buzzer in the hall.
Or is that another one?

VIOLET:
He's the boarder.

JACK:
The boarder?

VIOLET:
A boarder. You're looking handsome.

JACK:
Bunny!
    (*They kiss fondly*).
What's he doing? Who *is* he?
    (*She pulls away, withdrawing from him.*)
44

VIOLET:
Children wade on the receding shingle
   (staring off)
gaunt in their practiced grace. Mature,
they ape their elders and cavort like
pogo sticks in the advancing foam.
Where well-mannered aeroplanes and autos
serenely sail, on the yellow sand, children
ignore their own innocence. They've taken it all
in, and know how they want their backs broken.
   (Then she faces him bitterly.)

JACK:
I know all about the attractive distances and
the distraction that's more elegant than a knife.

VIOLET:
Never mind the rabbits and tears. You're
just as ruthless as anyone else.

JACK:
I thought
I'd want to play cards all night when I got home.
Listen, I know I'm stupid, I think for weeks
about things other people read in the newspaper.

VIOLET:
You may be dumb, but it makes you clever
because you know it.

JACK:
But I've been away.

VIOLET:
All those letters, so beautiful . . .

JACK:
I've been away,
that's all, I've just been away.

45

VIOLET:
. . . designed to upset
me sufficiently that I wouldn't be able to stop
whining about your absence until I heard the hoot
of the steamer bringing you back.

JACK:
It's still my life . . . .

VIOLET:
Fortunately I've always had a very strong sense
of responsibility for the happiness of others.

JACK:
You're still in it.

VIOLET:
I'm a veritable Florence
Nightingale of the heart, or as one of your old friends
once remarked, "She has a bit of the good-hearted madam
in her." You see, you haven't asked me the right
questions.

JACK:
Am I looking handsome?

VIOLET:
Why don't you ask
me if my slip fits?

JACK:
Has he been staying here?

VIOLET:
Or if the steam-fitters union still meets for
its annual picnic in Lewisohn Stadium?
    (JOHN *enters clothed.*)

46

JOHN:
Well, has my little Cio-Cio San told
the nasty Naval officer to scram?

JACK:
I'd like to have a word with you.

JOHN:
Let's have lunch together after you've found
yourself a job. I'm writing a novel your firm
may find itself interested in.
    (VIOLET *turns to* JOHN).

VIOLET:
I wish you'd
go away and stay away. All you've done is kept me
looking out windows, wondering what things were
really like. Get out!
    (But she throws herself into JOHN'S *arms and cries.)*

JOHN:
There, there.
    (He looks over her head at JACK.*)*
What have you done to my poor baby to confuse her?
Why didn't you send us a telegram to expect you?
It was quite a shock to see you. I never saw you before,
so you can imagine how it's tested my equanimity.

JACK:
Shock! I come home to find you both in your
underwear in this place that looks like the
landscape outside a bottle factory, and you ask
me why I'm not more considerate of the woman who's
been eating my brain for years in the salt mines
of the heart, its panic? That's where all the wars
rage, you know. That's where all the despatches
come from. It's never a matter of killing, it's
a matter of suffering, it starts blowing up.

47

I want her, that's all, I want her breasts
leaning into my armpit against shop windows on
Sundays, I want the empty smell of her flesh
in the morning when she's gotten up to go to
the bathroom, I want her whole open valley
breathing noisily when we're drunk in the wet
mist of dawn as the pennants begin to stripe
themselves and the wind whines towards the
suburbs. You can't have her.

JOHN:
You're wrong.
She wants me, because she's interested enough
to hurt me. Life went to the trouble of putting
me here in these old but well-worn clothes
that've seen better days and better hers
and never even wanted to go away and get fixed up.
You've got a claim on it, but I've got it.
These things don't happen temporarily.

VIOLET:
I love you.
(Against his neck.)

JACK:
What did I do wrong? What's happened to me? It's
like coming onto the stage, sitting down at the piano,
and finding no orchestra there! Why feel guilty, if
what I've done doesn't mean anything, if what I've said
doesn't move you? I held you in my heart, like a charm—

JOHN:
I suppose I'm the snake-in-the-grass but
I can't say I'm sorry. Someone has to smile
at her as she comes back from the bathroom.
Do you think everything can stay the same,
like a photograph? What for?
(JACK starts to exit slowly.)

VIOLET:
I would like to fill a jungle
with elephants and gorillas and
boa constrictors. I would like
to fill the trees and waterfalls
with the blackness in me, so I
might be a bird of paradise.

It would be fun to break a bottle
of wine and have it turn to water.
Or shoot a clay pigeon and have it
go honk! honk! and lay an egg in
the marshes. I'd rather not be
a wedding guest.

If I were the sphinx I could lie
in the sun and stare at myself
with pure white eyes. When I smiled
airplanes would go off their courses.
I'd hold down the dark and say
sweet nothings to the palms.
        (He takes her in his arms.)

JOHN:
Honey, I designed that costume for you.
You always look that way to me.
That's why I'm so mean.

(CURTAIN)

49

CHANGE YOUR BEDDING!
A Noh Play

To John and Judith Ciardi

First produced by the Poets' Theatre, Cambridge, Massachusetts, in 1951 with the following cast:

MAX, a boy	George Montgomery
LILLIAN, his mother	V.R. Lang
ALFRED, his uncle	Jack Rogers

Scene: *A library of no particular pretension or distinction, neither shabby nor elegant, rather dimly lit and comfortably furnished with divan, chairs, and books.*

Time: *Now or yesterday.*

ALFRED:
No one remembers such a winter. The
trees successfully beseeched the sky
for favors, and they fell down upon us
like pamphlets telling of chemical
warfare. The motors roared and we
could feel their powerful anxiety
wanting us to know the worst, until
we were covered by a great column
of snow and the motors were muffled
away.
  Then mother said, "The sleigh,
dad, can't possibly get through to
the Post Office, and we were expecting

51

the novels by Dickens for the children!
You must stay home from the office.
I'll mend." And immediately after lunch
night began to sneak towards us like
a wolf. We could hear it echo off
the barrage balloons.

        My little brother,
too young to fire a gun, climbed onto
the roof to play, and met there a
splendid smiling Tartar with red points
and bells on his boots. His skin was fat
and unintimidated by the snow. He sang
many oriental songs and taught my
brother a rope trick.

        But inside the
house was different. We were wet
through. Grand-aunt Elizabeth and I
played casino nervously, waiting to be
called for military service. The snow
didn't stop. It piled around us, velvet
by night, silk by day. Finally father and
I shovelled a path to the Post Office
and there I was fitted for a uniform
against the unparalled inclemency of
the weather. The worst in years.

        Returning
we found that the Tartar had broken into
the house and killed Grand-aunt Elizabeth.
As if both thought I'd never come back!
My sister, your mother, saw him. And the
next morning I did leave for the front.

  LILLIAN:
You don't have to tell me
this. I remember it all. I
remember that storm too well.
You went away to the war.
I'm the one who stayed and
cried and worked my youth
away in proper show of grief.

ALFRED:
I was telling the boy.

LILLIAN:
                    You
needn't bother. I'll tell him
what he has to know. I always
have, haven't I? He'll come out
all right. He will grow wise
by acting the way his father
would have had him act toward
me.

MAX:
Oh don't start that again!

ALFRED:
Remember the respect due your
mother; though we differ, all
three of us, in conversation!

MAX:
You know very well it's more than that!

LILLIAN:
He will listen to me because he must!

We first heard them at the great gate
muttering like burning swamp grass,

then in the streets they sounded like
hulls of the heavy fishing fleet. At night

they moaned but then we thought of wolves
and mothers and were not alarmed. Why,

it seemed we knew them: ambiguous voices
of a chorale we'd learned too early to

remember. Ah! my son, we were too thoughtful!
They were upon us, as near and disciplined

as a waltz, their chargers foamed at the bit,
their breeches gaped, their eyes were bloody!

    MAX:
I know these things,
Mother. I've listened
to you ever since I
can remember anything.
But what you tell me
is only a game or fairy
tale, though seldom
pretty. It's never really
happened to me like
things in the life I
am myself. You talk or
rant about your special
room, a favorite history
book that's already been
given its meaning. You
can't force my motives.

    ALFRED:
Lillian, let's stop this.
                  I wish you would.
To be sure each of us has
to make a fancy story out
of things, and it's always a
true tale. But no one else
can act on that information.
The map we made is only useful
for getting us about the city.
Anyone else would go wrong.
                  Even the fountains
have changed their design
and we thought they were
absolute tears. It's harder

to grow old this way, I know
                    as I should,
than if you fumble all the
way without a trace of knowing and are dazzled by order
at the end of the climb. But
you and I chose a different way,
eager to have reasons and a
guide. We made a success of it
                    but those mountains
changed as we approached, we
hadn't been thoughtful enough
is the trouble, although we did
a lot of thinking, and the
peaks were just other hills.
Let the boy alone. We could
have used those clouds. Who
knows what makes the grandeur?

LILLIAN:
You are not going to marry
this woman!

MAX:
          Try and stop me!

ALFRED:
Talk, Max! For god's sake say
something, explain yourself!

MAX:
I'm too angry to speak
now, here. And how could I
explain her to you when
I don't understand myself?
You're both so different
from me that my real idea
of beauty isn't plain.
She is everything. It's

55

not just her grey eyes.
None of her features
separately would go on
a statue. But she herself
is all the big important
things. When she gathers
herself together and moves
her eyes are an adventure
in the sky and her hair
falls like the sea. Her
voice moves over the earth
without singing, more
intelligible than music.
She draws me to her as if
she were beautifully veined
marble and I had an idea,
or as if she were a word
I hadn't yet pronounced
but had always longed for.

ALFRED:
She must be very beautiful
indeed, Max. I envy you
the dilemma. Be careful.

LILLIAN:
Dilemma! There is no dilemma.
She's a common slut! I've
looked into her. She's been
everything all right, but a
whore. She has neither the
need nor integrity for that!

MAX:
Mother, I'm glad you can be
so frank about yourself!

ALFRED:
Lillian! both of you!
this is an ugly scene

and only duty demands
I suffer it. What can I do?

MAX:
Let me tell you about me,
Uncle, it will be novel.
Everyone has thought they
knew for so long. Listen
for a change. I've been
living right beside you.
Always the quiet child
wrapped in his shell like
a dream, afraid of the
world because it seemed
foggy and haunted by
vague and sinister shapes,
And it was haunted be-
cause it was yours, not
mine. The rules were
yours, and the games, and
the real people. I had
to do my own exploring
and sinning. I fought
my own way out of my
self into the sun, so
how can you tell me what
any thing really is?

LILLIAN:
What a lot of nonsense!
You've always been petted
and spoiled, that's what's
wrong with you! I tried
my best to engage you in
everything we did. You
withdrew as if you didn't
know us. You could have
made our world yours, made
us happy. You are a cold
and willful son!

ALFRED:

                       Please,
Lillian, there are some things
we never want to see.
Proximity only seals
the blindness, and we
trample them like useless
flowers or the tag-end
of a day's outing. What
you are talking about
is a kind of death. Max,
tell us, tell us what's true.

MAX:
When I woke up my
mouth was full of
blood. It wasn't
funny. It wasn't
bats or vultures, I
hadn't been dreaming
of Leonardo. It was
my self. I leaned
out the window. "Stars!
go off your courses!"
and then tried to
smother in my pillow
but it got worse. All
over the floor. The
police came. "I don't
know" I told the doctor
but he was stern and I
saw clearly "it's my
whole life doctor, I
don't know when it
began." He was very
kind to me. And I
suddenly felt better.
As if I'd just reached
the North Pole and

wanted to go there.
I looked out the window
and the stars had come
closer. I knew then
that I could travel.

ALFRED:
But how?

MAX:
            She was
my nurse. She came to
me with pictures of
airplanes and secret
recipes for drinks. I
loved her from the start.
At night we would dance
on roof tops, right out
the hall door, and days
we flew over North Africa
or swam to Italy.
                        She came
to me each day like
setting sail for the
Orient; for the first
time my bed was art-
iculate. And
the ordinary things like
daylight wind and sea
became, yes, beautiful.

ALFRED:
My boy don't give this up, there are few
times in life when you'll be able to speak
this way, and believe me manner is all
it's love and knowledge and joy and life

the only way to look at things and know
what they are and what they mean. I'm not

just nostalgic for youth. These words are
you, defend them for they are your love.

MAX:
I meant them, uncle,
and you understood.
I am in the right.

LILLIAN:
You are trying to make me feel tired and wrong
and obscene, my boy, but you won't! I am the
logical sentence in your blood and all the rhythmic
words color and flesh in the world cannot alter
a syllable. This other woman's free form will fall
into patterns of light and shadow, upon them you
will gradually stand, stamping and shouting as
now, erecting elaborate structures of order and
deceit, which will only articulate my memories!
You will betray her as you betray the past and me!

ALFRED:
Lillian, you mistake the
choice and the chance. I
have known, though weak,
that your memories are
dreams of choked time, I
have watched their useless
tangle contort itself till
your choices now obscure
your very real disgust.
You are afraid to look
from the apparent horror
to the real pain, and I
fear with you. Neither of
us can guess what past
the future will find
useful. We have no right
to speak or to will.

MAX:
Desire has already chosen
her for me. Through her
body the earth beckons.
Her eyes are
            what the sky
eagerly mirrors. Mountains
are only predictions of
Venus as she walks. And
the future
            waits for her
lips to shape its beauty
from my error and my love.

[CURTAIN]

WHAT CENTURY?
a play

King
Page
Stranger
Chamberlain
Girl
Queen
Ingenue

Dowager
Benjamin Franklin
Creoles
Handsome Cajun Cockteaser
Horsedrawn Tram
Cathedral Chimes

Act 1

Waves breaking like bees on the shelf of Armorica, while the scent of burning almond leaves fills the nippled sky. All elegance seems to have set aside its mask so that the wandering troubadour in his coat of many colors, unlike the sunset, feels at home across the several seas and stays everywhere semipermanently. This buzz-saws into the mind as indifferently as the line of the horizon and as precipitously. Which of us has not cried "Bearings? what bearings?" at one time or another when disaster seemed to be gathering its bouquet for the maiden toss? To be alert is to be decorative. Winter.

KING:
I'm fatigued with being angry,
my country's always hungry.

Whenever I'm in doubt
the Minister of the Interior, tout
decorator and Casino connoisseur
resigns. Then I falter. An entrepreneur
with English schooling appears
from nowhere; inferior, but perseveres.
Years go by, the regime is stable
but for one General, irritable
and cologned, who has hoodwinked
the Queen, my grouse. The wall must be chinked
with her charming kinky hair
or a nunnish nation cries its disrepair.
At sunrise I'm prone and I weep.
My pride is a turnip.

> *The court, ermined and dovetailed, disperses and tallyhoes in view
> of a forest which darkly tiptoes backwards. This withdrawal is
> accomplished by the heavy-hearted ticking of sandpipers on shin-
> gle. A red mist descends.*

GIRL:
Who has passed the nuts to the Countess?
She has threatened to cut me with her diamonds.
Oh I am ill! I am afeared, afeared so. Mounds
of such surgically contaminated livers! Countless!

PAGE:
How dreary the girls are
when they prate,
cold like the Evening Star
so wet, so late

so lippy in exceptional parts
and not much frivolous,
their hemmed-up little hearts
seem marvellous.

I have kissed many coming
and all were humming.

QUEEN:
Run, run. It's all I do. Shall we make
the border? What's going on under darling curls?
whose flaccid Chinese-powdered cheeks' pearls
are about to be pressed breastward. A lake

of prurience's as good as a young fountain.
Where is the political emissary I sent to the Baptist
missionary to essay the pork chops? If it's a mishap, 'tis
the treacherous ladder of the lily-strewn mountain

of Restful-Party-Caucus, named by the Grand Vizier
of Viet Nam on his third and a half joy trip
west to the home of the bison and curd. King Philip,
the Indian bravest, blazed trails. What could be dizzier

than his famous Mohawk Romp, the motor
cavalcade touring Drive-Ins and Auto-Camps
and Swing-Rendezvouses and Firemen's-Ramps,
it's enough to be a Queen! One should be a daughter.

They dance slowly in harlequins and transparent dominoes. Are
extremely cheesey and informal. Delores, a lady-in-waiting, has
the rag on. The smell of citrus fruits unnerves the palmy air. A
Communist enters the Garden of Velours, smiling like a wallflow-
er outdoors. The first violin dissonantly gusts, for a moment only!
into a strain from the Missouri Waltz. Smile? how they all frown!

STRANGER:
Where can I get a pedestal made?

INGENUE:
Is "the divine Cecile" really Cecile Chaminade?

CHAMBERLAIN:
I have set out the linen and washed cups
to humble myself and render obvious
the meat of my worship of those ratty pups,

the Crown Prince and his Crownier devious
and gullible step-brother, Connie. No idea
is safe with those two beebee eyes. The carious

token with their withheld approval is a career
kneecap. I've been banged in the thighs
by both their set-up ears. A shell-pink ear!

any one of the four is capable of sinking my eyes
when it bells my breast. Hooded falcon which sups.

*He falls dead, the traitorous wretch! and the jade balloons flip into
the white sky. The sound of syncopated tickertape is heard down the
marble men's room of the Aerolinea Fanconiliana di Cilea. A
tray of sausage patties is brought in by an old lady.*

Act 2

DOWAGER:
Now why would anyone leave a plate of penises in the waiting
room of the Marrakesh Funicular? Starch my tail! if it isn't
an odd country, strange inhabitants! weird customs! What was it
Cicero said? I'm getting out of here. Bong!

Act 3

BENJAMIN FRANKLIN:
When to the pressures of the past
I summon up my legislative powers,
I 'nvisage lands in which the jujubes last
and drop upon the people from gay towers.

Talking with Alexander Hamilton at night,
whether alive or dead, in subtle seance,
we settled upon a ruse, a sequinned blight,
to keep the golden maize crop in abeyance.

Now I am old and for a little wheat germ
I'd give up sentimentality and take down
my lovely French lace to hold my seat, term
after term, wrapped to the ears with eiderdown,

in fashionable America. But it's too late,
the wheat sheaves are all in store windows
on hats, and what can you trade immaculate
urbanity for, when it has sinned, and owes,

and can't pay a sou? I'm in the wrong register
and the aria's too Alpine for my nose. I
thought, with poets, chic could be a Magister,
an Emperor! but ugliness erases my keen eye.

I insist! I insist! I sought for nought but beauty
and onion soup and chocolate, bored by duty.

*Silver light and the sound of a great gong stifled in windbells and
jewelry as Franklin sobs loudly in Italian.*

Act 4

*New Orleans at the Turn of the Century. A helicopter alights in a
field where some Creoles are smoking opium and complaining.
The music of De Falla. The word "Swanee" on a large blue bill-
board in the swamp. Natives dance with fans, swords and similar
appurtenances, all in color. A carefully selected pile of white eyes
lies in the center of a banyan grove. A wild boar routs among the
roots, snuffing the sweetness of the sweet potato, so orange, so rich!
A Creole hymn and much psalming it up in the bushes.*

Hymn

We done got ebbahthing but lub,
dat de thing we rootin ob,
ain no shame de King am ded
ain no shame de Queen in's bed,
an dat ole fart de lillil gull
am passin wet de Page's tulle
you cain tell me dat reddish mist
don mean dat somebuddy got kist
and pushed out on de dreary street
where Delores an de Communists meet
an de Stranger do it in a dooah
to dat suck-ass Ingenue, dat whooah!
dat lousy lay, dat Chamberguy ambidexterous
I tink he wah homosexterous

Ah's goan flay awah ah's goan flay awah
Ah's goan flay awah in de helicoptah!

HANDSOME CAJUN COCKTEASER:
Old wid de up, down wid de new, it sho ain New
Yeah Dah fo nuttin, ah sho hates rootin abaht de Fohest
    Primmivale
widout dey be sum soht ob owdiens. Dis tree heah done
    jus gib me
a gud drope ah dun goan gash hem propah an retun la-
    teh fo ah feel,
dat way ahll no hem bah de gleem in dose dahlin femi-
    niin eyen. It
am infinut, de fragrunt vuhsutilitee ob trees,

Ah goan to de citee to see whut ah be seen and whut
    beeyou-
teefill goan happun to di huppy lard. Grant gudness, ah
    bein
hensum an ahll an mah whait teef am a sun fo sho for
    ahll de

68

helfy yum fucks what dan mammy an pappy in de
 church, ah hopes
sho ah goan anjoy my seff cuz date ahll, dat ahll.

HORSEDRAWN TRAM:
Drrriiiiing! Drrarrrrlliiiiing! Tih!

CATHEDRAL CHIMES:
I have indeed, on this day, above all others, a hopeless
nostalgia for Paris. Let me count the days. May my tears
 fall as
rust and stain the People.

[1953]

MEPHISTO

A Cloud
A Multitude
The Watercress Troubadour

Act 1

One thousand eight orang-utangs in the corridor of the Hotel
Surprise. A pearl necklace falls on them. They die noisily.

Act 2

A CLOUD:
A vision has been spied
of loveliness in gypsyland
and no one knows what to do.
Do you? I took her by the hand
and she was cold to me and lied

like all the other spies.
I then thought her ordinary, wrong,
wasn't I? to think her out.
To shout. I felt her fire of tongue
stand straight against my eyes.

A MULTITUDE:
She is dammed, that dancer, for her lack of energy
and her understanding of arrivalism.
  When she was hired she was sighted, and not
before then. Do you think that she is a witch. Do
you? It is difficult to see which thing hanging in
the air she is, when you have no dime for the revolving
telescope. All the advertisements were wrong, I gave
her to my son and she was not the moon.

Act 2, Scene A

The sound of not-very-warm hair in curlers.

THE WATERCRESS TROUBADOUR:
I heard the wind of the
hounds, of the hounds into
the heart, the most musical ones. It
was a very giggly evening without
lights and I seemed a little older
than my photographs. No one would
tell me so, the blue lids of the lake.
I asked my dancing partner to take
a tub with me but there weren't enough
people at the party to make it worthwhile.

Act 3

I tend to think that the brevity of the season is that white
    recall,
that paramour in the distance who is always dancing
    while she waits,
you know. The scrubbing that the sailors hear. Do you
    know the

yellow will? It is tugging at my life, yet I hear only the far-
fetched pace-setters who are covered with hair. I regret them.

[NY 52]

VERY RAINY LIGHT,
an eclogue

Daphnis
Chloe

DAPHNIS:
Remembering at best bitterly
that peacocks are not a hit with
you. Chinchilla, you are beautiful.
All that you've given me's at one.
I'm not chilly thinking of bones.

CHLOE:
Someone has glued my castanets
together. And this morning early I
became aimlessly apparent cause
I woke up first and the dew jetted
from your armpits of ambergris.
I smelled burning rubber, I did
not receive a cable from your Europe
every[one] being at war at the time.

DAPHNIS:
All praise to Juno, she as disaster
cuts a fine figure. Your diamonds
are dripping like spit. Am enamored.

CHLOE:
The whistle of your gaze cuts across
my hair like spurs. You're the big
breeze in halflight, don't think I

don't know it. At dawn when I'm milking
the aphids I hear your stomach
coming up like thunder. Oh baby.

DAPHNIS:
Onto what Nizhni sifts, ja ja,
the appealing moo? Under which
nasty mummer skips the coral rope?
I like you, but perhaps you, fiery,
are no fit companion on field trips?

CHLOE:
You must come when my throaty heart
traces the wiry meteors to breathe
in your ear its invitation to the beach.
I will scare up the money to chase
you into my arms where, like winter
flowers, you'll find small sentiments
lunging robustly. Warm. Is as if
I am your sheeted will for windward.
I shall leave a jar of powdered coffee
on your tongue. Be wakefully mine.

DAPHNIS:
O joy! o joy! today's the day, eh?
I've quit pictures for the grassy knolls
of knees and apple of your nut.
No more greys for me! You. Artichoke.

CHLOE:
O infinite languor of railroads!
truly you master a heady scent.

[NY 5/52]

76

AMOROUS NIGHTMARES OF DELAY,
an eclogue

Teacher   Bob
Kenneth   Jimmy
John   Larry
Jane   Barbara

> "Well, and how have you been, Medea?"
> —John Ashbery, *The Heroes*

Scene 1, the playground of a New England schoolhouse, early spring. It is noon recess, and a few of the more fortunate children are munching snowballs. The students are of the assorted ages which fit into one room and they are clustered round their dear teacher, picking his brain.

TEACHER:
In my pocket? Only some old racing tickets from the
Narragansett tracks, "to show," saved by me because I
could not go that day, could not accompany my Dear One
because I had to take an airplane.

KENNETH:
But sir, when deliquescences spring from the front, on
the front! like little horns? I met, I mean, a

> Little faun from Zanzibar
> whose antics frowned adown
> the tramway to the pictures
> where the shadows kissed all

77

afternoon like silver leaves.
It was the faun's quarter!

Is there any sense in which this experience was truly beautiful?

JOHN:
Ahhhhhhh!

JANE:
Every day in every way we grow smarter and smarter. I
should live so long. Everyone gets to do everything.

TEACHER:
A deep one.

JOHN:
When I speak to you, I speak of the spiritual, which is
my fulfilling need. It opens to me, flowers unfurl their
gloomy banners to my appetite, readily, like a lunch box.
Sometimes I stare out the window as if I were drinking,
and it is at these times you become most annoyed, not as
you think because I am not attending you, but because
something is attending me which you are wary of the ex-
clusion of. Is it not true that the natural saint spends
her precious buddings masturbating, until that rich hour
when the voices will enfold her in that high distraction
which she has been seeking with closed eyelids and hot
cheeks? Then, beautiful borrowed eyes, you will find the
rough tongue of death wrench you like a daisy, you will
go green, there will be a fluttering but no dismay, you'll
be the feathered wing of a cloud. You don't know it, but
you will fall like rain.

KENNETH:
I have been misunderstood!

TEACHER:
If, indeed, anyone is ever misunderstood. I would like

78

to conduct a little poll: hands up, how many have seen a
woman naked?

LARRY:

What pseudo-kinetic response dins its palpitations into
my flapping breast? The wanderer like a gust of wind be-
devils me towards that role I can't run fast enough to
catch the coat-tails of. What is it John just said that,
like his life, finds me on the long distance phone? Women,
we all think of nothing but women, and the little thing
they have that they have not. For instance, whenever I
approach, so systematically! a crevasse, it's as if the
hanged man already swayed there like bell-buoy adrift,
catching my ear, always my ear! Is there no one else
intrigued by this particular spectacular death, which
like the wolves, is always smiling? It is like comic books,
I urge you, serious and verifiable on busses by bootblacks
and those who have gotten to walk that way on the brink.
I am as good at games as any of you.

TEACHER:

Ah, Jane has. But it is not the same for her, because I
suspect she won't admit she means herself; and I suspect
she has shown this same self to the boys, unmercifully.
Well, why not? she is wayward and smart and poetic, isn't
she dear? and will live to loft many a blue flamingo over
the waters of the despair of the times.

JIMMY:

It's to be hit on the head, to listen hard and wish to be
favored as the last of the ducks, the little trundler who
springs suddenly into the apple tree and starts eating
furiously. When I wonder you know what I mean, you know
what I mean, I don't want to see that the devil has me hand
in glove because then the exact opposite thing will happen
in a sheet of flame, a little time-capsule, so boredom will
be encouraged and, like a virtue, be already a habit. You
know what I lazily always order? the thing I like least, as

they usually go that way and you get it anyway when your
turn comes around and the signs are right like an axe. Gee,
Jane does stare sometimes. She doesn't even know what "zowie"
means.

TEACHER:
Sometimes you must buy your tickets after the train has
left. They call it "one of life's lessons," or at least
it's passed down to us, firmly and attractively imbedded
in tradition and gracious living and tact. You may wonder
any time you wish, even in class, about the form divine,
the "monotonous outline," and I shall never blame nor
reprimand you. Think of smoke, rounding a bend somewhat
ahead of itself, and slightly derailed.

KENNETH:
I am never pompous, sometimes I have to consciously avoid
stuttering, that's all. Nobody loves me, I wonder who?

*Scene 2, A rose garden and beyond, the sea. Invisible behind a
hedge, a monkey grinds a broken hurdy-gurdy. Our children are
now in their teens, the boys glamorous in knickers, Jane looking a
little disguised in simple muslin. From time to time one of the boys
heats a coin with a match and tosses it over his shoulder so it can be
caught by the monkey with a glad cry.*

TEACHER:
Now we are in strange territory, all the red flowers. You
must listen to everything that's said to you and you won't
get run over.

BOB:
Rearrangement and assessment continual and omniscient! If I
am to garden here I must have the absolute of my way, no
fiction tendered on a skewer by the factory. Barbara, leaving
the house at the minute to enter my retreat, will say "That's
where the money comes from," but what does she know?

JANE:
I tell you, I really mean it, there is something in the
country air, a fever as of roses, how obscure! In the next
life with a thousand grinning dahlias dripping honey on
my charred ankles I'll think pleasantly of this beach and
its rumpled vista, its good view, my unhappy heart. How
relaxing it all is! If we'd only been here in 1937 we could
have helped the Spaniards ashore. I deem cobalt the most
honest, I deem white the most frothy. My eyes are watering,
I'm going to sneeze and puke.

JIMMY:
When a remark is taken for excitement it means someone
intimate is missing. We ransom our catechisms with a
million malapropisms, but after all French really is un-
translatable, isn't it? Imagine covering all these blooming
ramblers with wet sheets! How glorious, that Barbara!

KENNETH:
Barbara will ride away on a Swedish bicycle before I get to
say "Sugar Ray Robinson," you bet. Oh! oh! my heart! the
gravel sounds like surf beneath her bare tendrils, she is
heavier than I'd thought.

TEACHER:
Be still, big boy.

JOHN:
Oh shut up.

JANE:
I don't think you ever did, you big phoney.

LARRY:
I want out, ugh! this open air, this plain air, this air!

JIMMY:
Run, all of you! The lawnmower! It's gone crazy!

81

LARRY:
I'm going to lie down. I want to have found the midnight
where my neck will be wounded. There, in the sweetness of
that pallid enclosure, with the anguished and inevitable
thirst that's quenched only by sand already beginning its
narrative of a life beyond cruelty and hobbies, I shall
rise like a tree and moan towards the void on glistening
runways in Oregon, pure as a paper mill. The fee that
once handed me a laugh will be sent me by postal money order,
for I'll be living outdoors and selling to be snotty, what
nobody needs. When "Easter" is read to me I'll know that
I've burst from the forehead like Minerva to be trouble from
then on for all concerned like any artist in the know.
On the Columbia River they'll build a shrine to me for
salmon, and those pink novenas once a year, in prestidigitat-
ing Spring! will cure crippled children of all but their
outlook and their beautiful eyes, withered forever in the
speeding glass of the rapids which I may very well, along
with everything else, who's to draw a line? become. And
the flowers all covered with paint and shit will throw off
the rot that began with my glances, those burning darts
I now think of as splinters, those needles I now shed like
stars. In my eyes they will always shine, and the little
ones can come to me, for it is better to be worse.

KENNETH:
I'm not running from no lawnmower.

TEACHER:
No, he's not.

BARBARA:
Now before this I had gotten some old lemonade, but I
didn't recognize you or what I'd thought you. How wide
the lawn, and how narrow the sky! Is is irresistibly
sucking us aloft like a high school? I want very much to be,
how do you say it? pragmatic, which in Bob's case is
furious. But you come at me,
you do, I can tell it, I don't hate you.

KENNETH:
Oh boy!

JOHN:
I discovered that girl, and I have wondered what happened,
as a mountain looks at the foothills and says "Come on!",
but her gaze, the deeper the better, tells me always to
take the next train for my grandparents who are dearest
and have lasted longest and are the last gentle things on
earth, lingering considerately like moss on the verge of
overpowering nostalgia which is a prescience of the infinite.
When to the darkening lense of their smile my being seems
a candle I kneel like a whole tribe, knowing that their
hoary gentility is the snow of the future already beginning
to vanish. Suns of my shadow! who made beautiful by being
old the rainbow trout of my selfishness, and recaptured me
while still an Indian, shedding their blood upon my knife
so I wouldn't be a novice. I could never have lifted that
hammock, yet lately I've moved it all over the lawn as easily
as a hatchet peels a cherry.

BARBARA:
Oh no.

BOB:
Go back into the garage, then.

KENNETH:
I have the right to claim blonde women like a mote of the
sun. I am over seven years old, but I have not relaxed a
single prerogative. Who has? as we are taught in Jeremiah
Joseph Callahan's "The Convict of Clonmell."

JANE:
We aspire, and we are continually more rescued by the ill-
temper of our activity, from day to day more openly hostile
to the circulation of the blood, which is always seeking
a way out, and would drip from the teeth of lap-dogs if
we were not, ah! so indifferently! the tough numbers we
delight in observing each other to be. The ivy, the scent!

Scene 3, A night club on the outskirts of town, near a highway thronged with trucks and their ilk. Colored lights rotating like someone sea-sick glance off the chromium furniture. The teacher lies in a bier in the center of the dance floor, and our kids, lavishly dressed, for they have inherited all their mentor's money, dance to a very fast fox-trot. From time to time they are frantically applauded by the patrons, who are occasionally lit up by the glancing lights.

ALL:
We thought to think it endless, the sudden brilliances of
his catarrh, which now that we are old and tired of hoofing
seems only elegant like an Edwardian newspaper. The worms
are already combing the feathered kimono we laid him out in,
and we had paid attention to nothing but our hardons while
a bowl of steaming hair was being taken away from the table.
I'm Jane, I'm Jimmy, I'm Larry, I'm Kenneth, I'm John, I'm
Barbara, I'm Bob, how are you, folks? we didn't know you
were there until just now so put the touch on us while you
can we're the forever fading into the future type of dancing
doll, yak, yak, it's the same as it ever was, you're all
from out of town, eh? baby, and that trap door there's not
just for the corpse, we've got to follow our little old
teacher into the dark where we spent the rest of our time
while you were waiting for us on street corners and in
peddlers' parlors, cause just cause we smile doesn't mean
the lights are going back on, get on your back or your knees
so your head won't come off when the trouble starts which is
like blowing up in a hot place say inside a pillow stuffed
with nylon vegetables for true nourishment and if everything
we say aint true the hereafter's going to wear us like a
stole, oh Mr. John! oh Miss Universe! all the intimate
revues agree it's snowing and your cars are safer parked
beneath Madison Square Garden where it's summer all year
round and the swans enchant millions with their "flightless
flights," so the newspaper columnists can get at us with
lemon forks and toothpicks we come twice a day in the arena
that's big time while intellectuals faint and a certain

smart somebody hones whatever he's going to use on all us public figures behind the wallpaper of the latrines in the Port Authority Bus Terminal which is inflammable by flash-bulbs: a big kiss to you out there. Oops! that's all, folks.

[END]

GRACE AND GEORGE,
an eclogue

Grace
George

Grace and George are showing themselves some scenery and history. The Alps are rising under them like escalators and their blond hair is tossing in the waves of an advancing sea of problems which, having been faced yesterday, seems only to have grown bolder. They have a very sweet attitude toward each other as if to say, "Well here we are", which however you will never hear that pair say, not if you listen by the hundreds.

GRACE:
Must you insist on wearing my old clothes! I thought
that at least when you got out of the army finally you'd look
a little less tacky.

GEORGE:
Why are you always thinking about "the" war? Look about
you: why must you always distrust the ease and variety of the
adjacent hills, whose volcanic inundations you claim are too
insistent, and peremptorily and characteristically you say
they deny the fatal scowl which appears like a mud pack on
the French face of what haunts us as beauty ?

GRACE:
I saw the waning tulip of night fade into a gossamer
shroud. I was all alone, and in that state you, suddenly as it
were and especially if no thought is already in your mind, ap-

preciate the particularity of all-ness and why it is always
coupled with human singularity in cosmic regularity.
(Sings):

> "I wander, you wondereth, that she doth roam.
> In loneliness my sinecure and my abode.
> I have not set my skirts upon the path of fame."

*The moon has meanwhile really come out as if summoned. The
sea wrenches at its moorings as in a geodetic survey chart held over
a candle flame, and edelweiss all around George and Grace, there
their eyes pop out a glittering blue of three-year-olds pierced by ar-
rows at summer camps. On the floor of the star-strewn lake where a
million hints of hibiscus whisper "Wordsworth!" in tune, where
the cats prowl in the rushes of dismay, a barge of twigs and hay
and shells plies carelessly its unwieldy wooden sail, creaks out the
message of perfunctory freedom and commerce, drawing uner-
ringly with its wavering wake across the faces of George and
Grace the frightful distinction of line between freedom which is
tartar and slavery which is self. "I had not cried these several
years." A tree topples down the slope and is planks on the silver,
frothing and sighing. "No more had I." And the crawling dia-
gram falters in the eye of human dispassion and grows less relent-
less upon the bosom of "The Maiden of the Roses."*

GEORGE:
Fame. How would she know you if you came?

*Now the wind has shifted, a breath of snow crumbles across south-
ern Italy towards the pair who, hand in hand, think only of sun-
sets. The delicate hair of a goat, slipping upon the glassy heights
and daintily painting the dizzy rants of green with his carcass,
crushes its spangling horns in the sand of the stippled water, spied
by a white-spouted steamer on the ocean far. How has our hero
wandered?*

GRACE:
Faster and faster pleasure has wounded me. As if its
mouth were mine, to be beseeched and not beseeched. I can,

at no carmine hour, remember the words the wizard said
would save me.

GEORGE:
Do you remember in far December how the spokes glittered
and wheeled and promised? I fainted near the door, knowing I was you, and you disappeared in charge of the cur-
rency which had risen, had fallen, on your own sable brow.
Could you have meant less, could you have trapped me and
forgiven me, could you have relented and freed me? Is that
the meaning of these faces in your eyes, the same faces
though infinitely varied and hung?

GRACE:
As once in the dark photograph where the two faces pon-
dered the floor, the one whose chin rested on the part
in my scalp, you must know that in our time the crowd
has gone home and the presses are silent, finger to lid.
I remember only the betrayal within myself which I sought
like a seed. Your claim is just, and will become a joke.
Why should not my art, which is highest, not rend us
both? My will is off the safety and, like a malarial
mist, our personal tombstones are wreathed with the iddity
of enormous circumstance, which is the substance of life.
See that prisoner of Chillon who committed the only crime,
the poetic crime.

*Now to be busy the streets have come out before dawn and run and
run and run, though never celebrating or alternating. All green
lights read "wait" and all red read "tell." A crisp hungness of the
Morning Star. When to the azure of our several beds we leave "our
private walks and arborways, common pleasures, to walk abroad
and recreate yourselves."*

GEORGE:
I have thought of those fabulous heroes who sank beneath

the h[e]aving torrents of Sardanapalus like a pleasure of
furs. Since there is no heaven you may summon all the
devils who amuse you across these anguished faces which
crouch and beseech. You could conceive the emptiness as
clarity, but who listens? who sees? It is as well to stroll
on the edge of an abyss like the great Atlantic; uncharted
it gave comfort to the last gargantuan sea-monsters, and
in the clear light of the oceanographer did not fail to
sink the Titanic.

In your wandering confidence you will soon find evil
imaginary and be proud of the creations of your only too,
now, accurate improvisation, thinking of death as existing
solely by your power of art; until one day in the forgotten assurance of the heel of the masters you will topple,
my poor darling, into a blackness which perceived your
insight and fed you and waited and did not weary of
your work, like a little girl who amuses her friends with
terrifying tales of robbers while Jack the Ripper is picking
the lock of the bedroom door.

GRACE:
Stick by me.

> Mercifully the clouds marshal their density and cover the waters as
> the great public life of our times, which has come out on the slopes
> of the mountains as it did in "The Miracle of the Loaves and the
> Fishes," falls sobbing on its earth. Adieu, my twins.

[2/52]

90

LEXINGTON AVENUE,
an ecologue

Amyntas
Doris

AMYNTAS:
O mournful sunset, I have lost
my sheep with the wandering blush
of the sun that would not linger
on my cheeks, not beyond noon. . . .

DORIS:
Sheep? you mean you've lost your
love, don't you? and your penis
is showing. Put that bunch of grapes
back on your lap. Just for dignity.

AMYNTAS:
Now that I am entirely disrobed
you feel flippant, don't you?

DORIS:
It's a compliment from me, don't
mistake my informality for disinterest . . .

AMYNTAS:
or do you expect me to forget the
cares of the day as soon as your eyes

Doris:
Never mind my eyes!

Amyntas:
                        open? It must
be the cocktail hour or you wouldn't
be up.

Doris:
    I've been up since dawn.

Amyntas:
                        No.
You are the dawn.

Doris:
                    Tee hee. I expected
you to take that tack. If you don't
understand something, you say I am it.

Amyntas:
Where are my beautiful sheep which
you do not believe in? I worry. Are
their delicate legs, somewhere, twisted?

Doris:
I don't disbelieve them, I've just
never seen them. You are very critical.

Amyntas:
I offer you these arms which have
protected animals, and these thighs
which have bumped them, and these lips
which have loved them as I love you.

Doris:
And I accept the man, for who
does not love all, cannot love me,
though it pains me not to be unique
and I would be the only animal

who ever rested, bleating, in your arms.

AMYNTAS:
But do you sense a terrible feeling
in the West?

DORIS:
                    But do you love me
least?

AMYNTAS:
    I love you only, though I
watch out for lots. For instance,
have you ever seen a sonata?

DORIS:
                        They
say the sheep are always describing

AMYNTHAS:
Well not to me!

DORIS:
                a sonata. Can it be
the lost sonata?

AMYNTAS:
                Can it be the lost
subway?

DORIS:
    Why aren't you more serious?

AMYNTAS:
I'm too worried about my duties
as a shepherd, and besides, lust
makes one frivolous.

DORIS:
            O does it? lust?

AMYNTAS:
You are describing my inner nature.

DORIS:
You are describing me with your arms.

AMYNTAS:
I am in love.

DORIS:
I am in love with you.

AMYNTAS:
You are becoming everything to me.
I love you more than duty, most
for looks, and more than hillsides
covered with their own plangent fragrance
which is just as much from bottles.

DORIS:
You adore me, don't you?

AMYNTAS:
Like
an animal!

DORIS:
I am a pasture for your
flocks.

AMYNTAS:
And I am grazing o'er
your citified blue locks

BOTH:
which now
are heaven in the metropolitan gaze,
for all that's duty and desire is dust.

[4/14/54]

94

AWAKE IN SPAIN

Magistrate
Flamenco Dancer
American
Village Mayor
Little Girl
Mother
Church Steeple
Generalissimo Franco
Hollywood Make-Up Man
Joan Crawford
Othello
A Sheep
Another Dancer
The Slap
Larry Rivers
Cemetery
Animals
Brook
Nightingale
A Boy
King
Duke
Serving Maid
A Statue of Delores Del Rio
Grand Vizier
Sodom
Count
Soldiers
Italian Diva

Two Shepherds
Sheep
Grandmother
21 Demons
King's Son
Peanut Vendor
Funicular
Messenger
Grand Vizier's Ghost
Baby
Mariner
Sail
Laura Hope Crews
Serving Boy
Courtier
A Widow
Court Barber
Princess Marie of Rumania
Harry Crosby
A 1936 Chevrolet
Admiral
Cassandra
Marlene Dietrich
John Adams
Benjamin Franklin
William Blake
A Cloud
King's Younger Son
A Telephone

Forester
Nurse
Gardener
Village Girls
Butler
Landscape Architect
Tourist
Crown Prince
Balcony Rail
Swallow
Prop Man
Village Flapper
Milkmaid
His Mind

His Soul
Turandot
Lytton Strachey
Mummers
Arshile Gorky
Soprano
Megaphone
Kenneth Koch
Grover Whalen
Spanish Refugees
Empire State Building
Reporter
Thomas Hardy

Part I

Act I: *A sky filthy with bangles, but soft, somehow, and pensive. There is a verdant meadow upside down in the center of the stage and many unhabituated animals stroll about, as if at a fashion show. A large pair of lips, greasily rouged, smile from the rear wall.*

MAGISTRATE:
Why are you so pensive?

FLAMENCO DANCER:
Oh lordy, it so wet!

AMERICAN:
Had you really been wholly mine at night
the fort wouldn't be sneaking its alarms
across the border like a saffron bite
or the tea lady keep nagging "Love harms"

every minute of the day and damn night.
I told you never to mention my arms
to Moors at Headquarters. My dear, be bright,
and never put your dope in candy charms.

Stay away from the soldiers every night,
Try to imagine what it's like on farms,
for in pursuing a Chrysler of white
you'll find tears in solution in your arms.

It was not to be so easily charmed
that we sent you to school to be harmed.

VILLAGE MAYOR:
Oh Iberia! You're weeping!

LITTLE GIRL:
Tra lalala la la la la la la lala la la la.

MOTHER:
"Carmen."

CHURCH STEEPLE:
Aoua! Crash! Bong, bong, bong, bong, bong, bong, bong.

MOTHER:
"Boris Godunov."

GENERALISSIMO FRANCO:
I'm so worried about the jails, they're full of Thanksgiving
dinners.

HOLLYWOOD MAKE-UP MAN:
Do you have a *Times*? You should just see yourself! You're
a perfect sight! I think I'll hire a touring car, are
there any clean ones?

JOAN CRAWFORD:
Ummmm, ummmm, ummmm.

97

MOTHER:
"Estrellita."

VILLAGE MAYOR:
Oh CARE package of delight!

OTHELLO:
The whole damned country is like a pillow.

A SHEEP:
I say there!

ANOTHER DANCER:
Stay away from the Spanish dancer as a type, señor. I've
lived in Tallahassee, tee hee hee. I'm warning you, old
pal, beat it. Tell the gauchos you saw me and I said "Okay."

VILLAGE MAYOR:
I don't care for your conduct. Here's a slap. Ugh, I can
hardly lift it.

*   *   *

Act II: *Twilight, seventeen years later. The animals are notice-
ably aged, the lips no longer smiling. The verdant meadow has
righted itself somehow.*

THE SLAP:
Come of age, damn you!

*   *   *

Act III: *The gardens of the Knights of the Garters of Spain. A
rippling brook flows through the center, sounding like a minuet.
At left stage rear a huge statue of Dolores Del Rio. Oh night, staring nightingales! trees hung with hemp! prunes! Madeira bis-
cuits! jumping blue blazes!*

98

Larry Rivers:
Where's the cemetery? They say there's a terrific cemetery around here somewhere.

Cemetery:
Here I am, Larry.

Animals:
Watch out! Boy, you almost fell in.

Brook:
Damn those busybodies!

Nightingale:
Thank heaven he's saved himself! His decorum is my sight!
On flute of an American, you are being beauteous.

* * *

Act IV: *One of those Spanish palaces full of ropes, artichokes, globes, and flames. Or is that Portugal? Very baroque. A little girl is being mistaken for a bull by the Italians in the courtyard. Night again. No, midday.*

A Boy:
Basta! Basta!

King:
Fabulous indeed are the charitablenesses of the table!
What gong so distinctively loud as the dissonant stomach?
I pray you, put down your feather duster and don't be
such a cat!

Duke:
You told me to take care of everything.

Serving Maid:
I wish Mister Mozart would hurry up and finish this.

A Statue of Dolores Del Rio *(offstage):*
I'm coming, I'm coming,
though my head is bending low.

Grand Vizier:
Oh my darlings! I've just written some marvellous new
letters of help to the art world so they'll get straightened
out. From now on Velazquez' shows will be reviewed in
the *Herald Tribune* and *Art News* has promised to do a
"Zurbaran Paints a Picture" in the fall. Isn't it
heaven to be a Sodomite?

Sodom *(offstage):*
Why is it all blamed on me? It's like associating sewage
with Venice!

King:
What a wonderful day it is! Wish you were here! And my
subjects all so happy. Look at those smiles. They all look
like Hapsburgs. Those pointless smiles, the very smile of
a Hapsburg. What's for banquet tonight?

Count:
Nothing, if the matadors don't have more luck.

King:
Hey, who's that running towards us?

Count:
It's the queen. Or is it the cardinal?

Grand Vizier:
It's meeeeeeeeeeeeeeeeee!

King:
Off with his head!

Soldiers:
Okay, king!
100

ITALIAN DIVA:
What a divine country!

* * *

Act V: *Is there a place known as "high in the hills of Granada"? I hope so!*

TWO SHEPHERDS:
We love the country, that's why we're handsome, it's love love love love love. We only quarrel over sheep. We're terribly natural, aren't we? Well, is the sky blue? What did you expect, a couple of Air Force Cadets? Not that we couldn't if we wanted to!

SHEEP:
Sure you could.

GRANDMOTHER:
Would you boys like to take sandwiches to school or come home at noon?

KING:
I'll get back into that palace, I know I will.

SHEEP:
Sure you will.

* * *

PART II

Act I: *A demonic height in Granada, a sun with 103 spots. Twenty-one demons are lined up on a mountaintop.*

1: I could hold this cigarette hanging from my lower lip for years, I know.

2: It's a tornado of logs falling on the pianists' wrists.

3: I would like to stay on this bus laughing with you forever.

4: The landscape is already finished, ready to be shown.

5: And holding her cheeks together were these splinters of glass on platinum spokes, except that she couldn't laugh comfortably.

6: Who laughs? O childhood, haven't you had your vengeance? Aren't you a Spanish boredom?

7: "Donald's Garage" keeps blinking off and on, in the silence of night.

8: I didn't know you were Jewish, I'm glad to say.

9: Thanks.

10: Does she have a pocketbook in her left hand?

11: The tree is turning white.

12: I am shifting with passion like a concert waltz.

13: The flowers don't seem to want to leave her alone.

14: Garrulously final.

15: And if we were statuesque we would be truer.

16: I saw myself in the mirror. I am one of those gargoyles that supports with his head the balustrade of the grand stairway the Cossacks charged up at midnight.

102

17: You savages aren't so inventive.

18: And there was someone whispering "To dissemble is to instruct," like a waterfall.

19: He is most anxious about his freedom when it is most complete, o tulip!

20: The most ecstatic praises on the shore!

21: Daylight clarified for me the loneliness of the razor and the elevation of the ill, the marriage of pretence and custard, the blossoms.

ENSEMBLE:
Yes, it is too late already; you are a man.

KING'S SON:
Who? Me?

PEANUT VENDOR:
What lake is that laying its head on the waterfall?

KING'S SON:
Yet, I shall not be discouraged. I shall recover my father's palace for the Old Man. All he needs is a few rooms to restore his health.

KING:
Attaboy.

GRAND VIZIER'S GHOST:
How it burns me! the black laugh of loyalty. It was worth dying to get this second hand.

ENSEMBLE OF DEMONS:
Hah! You'd need an army.

KING:
He will not.

SHEEP:
Where am I? My nose is bleeding.

STATUE:
Go down, then.

FUNICULAR:
I'm like an angel, ain't I? Look, everybody!

DUKE:
It's a revolution! Boy, am I glad I'm not around the court.
Better to be an exile than be exiled. It's a revolving door,
damn it. The late duchess, my wife, used to say, "Look,
it's moving" as if she'd never seen a member before. Well?

MESSENGER:
Which way to His Majesty?

DUKE:
Thataway.

KING:
Who was that?

SHEEP:
Sure it was.

GRAND VIZIER'S GHOST:
Haha! And they say there's no jeunesse doree. Waldemar will
be furious.

BABY:
Here I am!

KING:
Throw him overboard!

104

SOLDIERS:
Okay, King.

* * *

Act II: *The trough of a wave somewhere off the Iberian Peninsula. Lunchtime, and the clink of ice in glasses. Muzak.*

BABY:
Wahhhhhhhhhhh!

MARINER:
Here we go again, my poor little smack is full of them already and it isn't four in the afternoon yet. Where will I put the fish and the fish oil? There you are, my man.

BABY:
Mama.

SAIL:
Uh oh.

* * *

Act III: *A brilliant ballroom hung with wigs. Yesterday, and very rainy, blustery, you might say. Strains of Rachmaninoff's "Rhapsody on a Theme of Paganini" caught between two elevator doors midway of a fortnight of sex. A great green face resembling the ghost of the Grand Vizier peers in at each of the many windows like so many chandeliers that haven't been invited.*

LAURA HOPE CREWS:
My dear, you're as talkative as Nijinsky.

VILLAGE MAYOR:
Don't try to be poignant.

GENERALISSIMO FRANCO:
How do you do? I'm wearing, how do you call it? Ry-Krisp?

SERVING BOY:
Ouch.

KING:
(disguised as a Negro singer)
Slogging through the mud
can yuh spare a nickel, bud?
De King am sinkin' fast
he forgettin' all de glorious past
who gonna bring um back?
who gonna?
hey nonny no.

COURTIER:
Oh mercy! ha ha ha ha ha!

A WIDOW:
They say the two of them are living on a mountain and
that the young Crown Prince Frank is marvellously sweet
to his dad. The perverse are always such opportunists.

GRAND VIZIER'S GHOST:
I like to think of the king going through with it as a
boring ritual and Frank enjoying it quite a lot.

COURT BARBER:
That's as it may be. Let's go swooning in the sea!

PRINCESS MARIE OF RUMANIA:
Meiner Liebling! meiner Schatz!

HARRY CROSBY:
The sun! the sun! the sun! the sun! the sun!

A 1936 CHEVROLET:
I can't wait to lavish my aspirations on the routes. What
a trailblazer I am. Remember Toledo?

ADMIRAL:
What? Harumph! Who's that painting a circle round the
Generalissimo's feet? Hey!

DUKE:
(disguised as a candle)
It's the famous Portuguese warrior, George Hartigan!
This means foreign intervention!

CASSANDRA:
(disguised as a messenger)
Cry Arrowroot! And let slop the Madeleine of legs!

GENERALISSIMO:
Yipe! Follow me! Call out the civilities!

KING:
(disguised as Joan of Arc)
No! Follow me! Off to France, and just in the nick of
time! Where's that dinghy?

MARLENE DIETRICH:
Now, boys.

COURTIER:
A musical saw! The greatest weapon of all. Gimme that!

MARLENE DIETRICH:
You brute! Take that!

COURTIER:
Ouch!

KING:
Attagirl!

MARLENE DIETRICH:
Come on, King, we'll fight from Paris! Where is your
darling son, the Prince?

KING:
We'll pick him up as we run through Granada. Let's
leg it!

MARLENE DIETRICH:
You darling. So droll.

*   *   *

Act IV: *Alarums and excursions. A horrible stormy day in winter
in these 13 United States.*

JOHN ADAMS:
Won't sign the Declaration of Independence? You French
pervert and fat man!

BENJAMIN FRANKLIN:
Okay, I'll sign.

WILLIAM BLAKE:
Oh my dear ones! Someday I'll make a pecan pie of your
thoughts.

A CLOUD:
I can't hear a thing for the noises and alarums. Something's
rotten in the Pyrénées.

SHEEP:
You'll hear soon enough.

*   *   *

Act V: *A fandango, in which dwell all the Spanish thoughts of ex-
iles. The simple liberation of tense, clarifying their nervous disor-
ders, makes them terrific dancers, being totally unselfconscious because of their preoccupation with the futurity of the past. Lavender*

108

drapes. A tiny wire table with an egg roll and a bottle of absinthe on it. Tears flowing down the walls, and a marimba in the center of the stage with several people napping on it.

KING'S YOUNGER SON:
Dad's asleep. Don't wake him.
The sun's gone out of our life,
it's better to be asleep. Life
gets you nowhere if you're him.

GRAND VIZIER'S GHOST:
What's happening? Oh! I can't bear not to know what's happening!

A TELEPHONE:
Excuse me! What number were you calling?

* * *

PART III

ACT I: *A dreary château outside Perpignan. Fifty-three old care-takers have been stuffed into a blue bathing suit with white piping and sidelaces and are hanging from a plane tree by their thumbs. Oh boy! It's August, and the runners from Spain are dropping dead on the routes. Will the news get through? each cloud is asking itself, hoping to be "found" by Boris Pasternak. The daylight is particularly intense this day. Thundering dried-up fountains.*

FORESTER:
How does it go now? Ummmmm? "Yoiks! Tally-ho! A-hunting" hum? "We'll" what?

NURSE:
Hey there! Don't you see this window's open? Shut up, now!

Silenzio! The Crown Prince is feeding his gold fish! Do
you want him to get his hand bitten off?

GARDENER:
He's become a terrible degenerate, from sadness.

VILLAGE GIRLS:
Oh the red suns, tra la.

BUTLER:
Isn't it like Sevilla during fest?

LANDSCAPE ARCHITECT:
An orange sky, with a white band about its throat, and
perhaps a sunken pool of black?

TOURIST:
It's another case of nature imitating Alfred Leslie!

CROWN PRINCE:
I once dreamt of appearing on a balcony like this,
but to multitudes. How glad I am I made a recording
of the dead Queen, my mother, playing this nocturne.
Each time I hear it the sky lowers and the day sinks
its feathery head against my shoulders and sobs.
Oh fountains! You are too ridiculous! Where are you?

I am working against time hoping against hope
that the King, my father, won't expect me to go back
to Spain until I've finished my "Complete Works
of Jean Genet in Spanish Translation the First Time";
and anyhow I haven't reinstated the monarchy yet,
hélas, I mean, caramba! My spies have forgotten how
to write.

Why is everyone always at me for something or other?
Even the Grand Vizier's ghost calls every morning, dead
these ten years. Well, it's the price of talent,

110

as exhausting as climbing a tree and then climbing down.
When I think of my childhood in Onset, Massachusetts.
Ah!

BALCONY RAIL:
How firmly he grasps me! I'm glad I gave up the trumpet
vine, though it broke his heart, poor withered fish. I
always hankered for a prince, glamorous rail that I am.

SHEEP:
Boy, am I exhausted! What a trip!

KING:
Hi, duckums!

SWALLOW:
What distinguished face is that plucking out the window?
with bars on it?

PROP MAN:
Didn't you know cognac was brandy, queenie?

SHEEP:
I feel better anyway.

VILLAGE FLAPPER:
I represent the Marilyn Monroe
fan club of South France, chapter one. Today
down below we are having a big row,
in her honor we are making some hay.

And are giving a banquet of shad roe.
Our darling's shooting a pix on a quay:
we're celebrating in advance her show,
which has a marvellous score by Sauguet.

Her "native wood-notes wild" are what we'd do
almost anything for, believe you May!

111

She makes us feel like an old Spanish shoe.
but that's better'n being bored at a play.

She is our love, yes, we love her, we do
and so should you and you and you and you.

MILKMAID:
Jeepers! Are you a "fire and ice" girl?

*   *   *

Act II: *Byzantium, the mid-century Byzantium of icecream cones, floating in lagoons and short, squat scientists investigating lunar eclipses over the Hebrides, the Hebrides Overture, I mean. W.B. Yeats is standing in the middle of a through-street in galoshes with a bad sore throat. His mind and His Soul are contending. A parade goes past, inescapably alert. The billboards look like dirty handkerchiefs and an art colony has "sprung up."*

HIS MIND:
Did you say a chaise lounge or a shared lung?

HIS SOUL:
The seas are full of fish from Spain. What a busybody I am!

TURANDOT:
I am not so successful in this country.

LYTTON STRACHEY:
It is a parenthesis I seek.

*   *   *

Act III: *The House of the Dead, Valencia. Greco's noted "View of T." executed entirely in red is used as a backdrop and brilliantly lighted. A lot of tubs full of Ma Perkins roses sitting around.*

MUMMERS:
Hot shit! It's terrific fun to sit around and read Italian
novels of Social Consciousness all the time. Hey ho.

ARSHILE GORKY:
It's terrible under Kay Francis' armpits.

SOPRANO:
"Dove sono," et cetera

* * *

Act IV: *Times Square, New York. Multitudes of holiday noise-
makers. A parade goes past, inescapably alert. The word "Zowie"
keep going around the Times Building in lights.*

MEGAPHONE:
The Crown Prince has reinstated the monarchy, but IN
AMERICA! MEXICO CITY HAS FALLEN! Your
correspondent, K. Koch, barely escaped with his life to
tell you the tale.

KENNETH KOCH:
Nope. Sorry, folks. They got my dispatch all wrong. It
all happened in Spain. I heard about it in Mexico, you see?

GIRLS:
Oh my darling!

LARRY RIVERS:
I knew Frank would do it! He's American through and
through.

KING:
Yes! Yes! I can hardly wait to go back.

GROVER WHALEN:
Here's your ticket, your highness, I mean, your majesty.

113

SPANISH REFUGEES:
(in native costume)
O joyous day! O joyful hour!
O boresome banana! O tripe!

EMPIRE STATE BUILDING:
Luncheon is served.

* * *

Act V: *An elaborate state picnic on the Rock of Gibraltar. The heat of the day. In the background, military maneuvers.*

REPORTER:
My paper is extremely interested in your point of view, sir.

KINGS YOUNGER SON:
Well, as soon as they got back into Spain and everything started to go okay, they decided I couldn't leave school in Switzerland even though I am forty years old.

GENERAL:
So . . .

KING'S YOUNGER SON:
. . . we attack the mainland in the morning. The Crown Prince will be bombed out of his Barcelona brothel before dawn, and then the putsch! God, it's wonderful to be in the field. Just look at them banners! Russia and Italy are on my side, France and America are backing the Legitimists, ho ho. By God, they're in for a tumble.

THOMAS HARDY:
O dynasties, incessantly tumbling!

[CURTAIN]

[NY February & March 1953]

114

A DAY IN THE LIFE OF THE CZAR
a play
(Hommage à Glinka)

Peasants	Czar
Cossacks	Nadejda Von Meck
Courtiers	Eucalyptus Tree
Modeste Mussorgsky	Anna Karenina

Act I: *Dashing and, even from a distance, incredibly fierce Cossacks are galloping down a mile-long avenue of peasant heads which, to one's astounding relief are seen to be dummies. To the right an Ice Palace lit by orange bulbs, tulips or some such, to the left an elaborate wooden church with a train station beside it and on the platform a sign reading* HARTFORD: in the distance the Connecticut River winds towards the White Mountains. No snow, but a certain heaviness of atmosphere, as if the next scene might be laid in Siberia.

PEASANTS:
Let's have the "Firebird Suite"! to Hell with Scriabine!

COSSACKS:
And they wonder why we're riding roughshod down this Boulevard of Open Seams.

COURTIERS:
We want Scriabine and we're right.

MODESTE MUSSORGSKY:
Let me at them church bells. I'll disperse the rabble.

115

CZAR:
I think we'd better let Piotr Illyitch do it. He has that
1812 verve that's such fun.

NADEJDA VON MECK:
He's just as good as Alban Berg.

EUCALYPTUS TREE:
It's so cold! Why did I get off that train?

ANNA KARENINA:
It's not the weather, my dear. It's an emotional
climate. It forbids us to put forth our leaves, drop them,
and fall down, like a lot of diamond bracelets. Take my arm.

(They exit, followed by the court.)

Act 2: *A performance of Puccini's "Turandot" in Russian at the
famous Bolshoi Theatre, after which:*

EUCALYPTUS TREE:
Thank you so much! what a marvellous way to spend three
hours.

ANNA KARENINA:
It was nothing, dear. Wait till you see "Parsifal."

[Southampton 1/54]

116

SHOPPING FOR JOE

by Frank O'Hara and Steven Rivers

*By Steven & Frank
& with Grace in it.*

Steve
Frank
Grace

STEVE:
I don't think you should buy him a present. He isn't worth it.

FRANK:
I don't think so either, but he'd be very mad if we didn't.

GRACE:
You're talking about the man I love.

STEVE:
The man you love? I never heard such a silly thing in my life.

GRACE:
What's so silly about it? I'm crazy about him.

FRANK:
What's so great about him?

GRACE:
His eyes. They're as beautiful as a hedgehog.

STEVE:
I think he should be cut up for meatballs.

FRANK.
In that case, let's get him some spaghetti.

GRACE:
I'll see you later. I'm going over to see him and tell him all the
bad things you said about him.

FRANK:
Oh don't go. We can't bear that.

STEVE:
Why do you like him? He's not goodlooking is he? He's not
strong is he?

GRACE:
Never mind. I have a secret.

FRANK:
Maybe it's because he likes you.

GRACE:
No he doesn't like me, but I chase him all the time. I
try to put his arms around my—

(Sound of a siren.)

FRANK:
Your what?

GRACE:
Oh never mind.

STEVE:
Well what are we going to get him? A lollipop?

118

FRANK:
A light bulb?

GRACE:
A television tube?

STEVE:
I got it. We'll get him a rocking horse.

FRANK:
No, he'd wear it out the first day.

STEVE:
What happened to Grace?

FRANK:
I guess she disappeared in that expensive sports store.

GRACE:
Sob, sob. Oh dear, I just got him a precious little barrel
for him to practice on, but it broke. Boo hoo.

STEVE:
You should have got him a bat and ball. He could bat himself on the head and throw away the ball.

FRANK:
I'm going to get him a barbeque set. Pretty soon he'll
have a family and they can eat outdoors all the time.

STEVE:
And guess who the wife is going to be?

GRACE.
I'm going to get him a crib to put his triplets in.

FRANK:
Good old Joe.

GRACE:
Yes, he's so sweet I will marry him for his money.

STEVE:
Yes, he's so handsome that all the girl hedgehogs honk
at him as he goes by

THE END

KENNETH KOCH,
a tragedy

by Frank O'Hara and Larry Rivers

Goldie	Tom Hess
Chorus	John Myers
Mother	A voice
Kenneth	Jackson Pollock
Cherry	Milton Resnick
George	Lewitin
Franz Kline	Yvonne Thomas
de Kooning	Philip Pavia
Paul Brach	Ad Reinhardt
Elaine de K	

A dark stage. Sounds of female groaning. The lights come up and three ugly girls are revealed standing and sitting in the center of the stage. They are the chorus. A garden. Sunflowers. Oppressively hot.

GOLDIE:
Maple veins! Yaphank! Frog's bottom! Motor's gypsy-strains! Contraction of cow-flop! October in Utah! Why has the city failed to produce a Chaucer? This a Jew did whisper in my ear, o wandering O of my dissonant clap-heavy knee-cap! When I swam in Bronxdale I knew all the fishes, I said, "Hello, girls!" and they trembled in their lockers.

CHORUS:
How are you, Goldie? Why are you sad? How can you talk? Who are you?

121

GOLDIE:
I have shed my skin like wind. I have changed my name to
Jack. When I masturbated I didn't say "mother". I said,
"Bluebells! be in my head" but the eye lubricant didn't work. I
had my nose put where my adam's-apple was. I exchanged
my anger. I got off the escalator. I killed my older sister and
became a Bible. I threw the wildest flowers in my cunt. Yum
yum I said to the colored elevator man but he finished what I
began. I pissed on the geraniums and watched them grow. I
favored the Yanks. And still he wandered under the Great
Atlantic Rainway, enjoying frigidaires near Carolina, elephants under homosexuals, everywhere decorating the drain-
pipes with "of"s, "oh"s, "as"s. "sub-beet's wrists", "mudge"s,
"ughlf"s, "slush's yoyo"s, "cuckoo-clock"s and "Chanukah"s.

CHORUS:
Do you wish you were a Gentile? Or a bathroom?

GOLDIE:
Spit curls. Alabaster hankies. Elephants from noses. I Rhi-
noed my ear lobes grey in spring. Men mistook me for January. Rectal mirrors. How I screamed! White. His eye groans
moved from navel to bloomers. I cooked a perfume. Hand.
Slender. Silken Venus undid my pinks. O that black and
white of Ken and me. In front of "Our Prizewinning Sneeze."
He hardly tells me. Love is the hand of going away. Solo. Yes
I'm as they've said: "Hung".

CHORUS:
Comb your hair with spinach. Wear Albatross eggs. A man is
a tongue.

GOLDIE:
I don't know why I do him but I do. In the Spring Song of my
·heart he is Mendelssohn. He has changed the birds. He has
the hands of a money-man and the lips of a leopard. He
speaks to me in three languages.

MOTHER:
Goldie.

CHORUS:
Goldie, your mother's calling you.

GOLDIE:
Mother, at night the sea speaks to me with Kochean over-
tones.

MOTHER:
He may be a spring song to you but he's a pain in the ass to
me. What a beau, he's an ape.

GOLDIE:
You don't understand, mother; he's beautiful in his way.

MOTHER:
I understand, I've been to the zoo.

GOLDIE:
Listen to this mother:
"We undress orders to Doris the day tobacco-lift, who
Senator, isn't that a movie star coughing in your turnip?
O cradle frost, wigged, crane-blowed, sign below Kentucky
That the Wettmay be white, dropping alleys on teats."
That's the side of him you didn't know.

MOTHER:
Maybe you should marry him, Goldie.

Act 2, Scene 1

*The Cedar Tavern. A day in June. He has just come from the air-
port, and has been repeating "Oh bag" for the past five minutes.*

KENNETH:
Oh bag! June makes the head run. When I think of all the water in Greece!

CHERRY:
What water?

KENNETH:
Hotel rooms in Saint Germain des Prés, how I loved renting the Aspirin Suite for a month! But it's terribly continental to be back, isn't it?

GEORGE:
Beer, Kenneth?

KENNETH:
I must admit my callow. Those sandy years in Cincy! My theme song. Boom. "I didn't know from nothing." The heat of being Jewish. The delicate cultural heritage of Avondale, like a nail in your shoe, comes smelling up my dreams. Oh Lily! oh mother! oh youth! why did I ever cross the water?

GEORGE (*disgruntled*):
Well, four-eyes?

KENNETH:
To run from Goldie? the fags I knew at Harvard? the Dread that gnaws me like a glacier? or Nancy, married in a rice paddy in Charleston, North Carolina, and not even to a negro? any one of these would have made a hairy ape out of an athlete. Or was it the loopy lips and breasts of Robin, always strumming on her old banjo? or was it Pat Hoey's intelligence that drove me East? the little darling who visited me in the dark and left in it, those Irish eyes, those wet fingertips, that chicken tongue, that changeable hair, that Syrian siren, now married to a Man of Science? On the plate of life, happiness is the greatest developper. Bong! I used to think she'd made a mistake, like the rest of them, but travel has widened me. (*humming*) Oh, les oiseaux sont gris . . . Aussi les

124

loups . . . I wonder if John Myers has persuaded Wystan to
make me a Yale Younger Poet yet? . . . The simple tears of
Liz Lerman honking through the El, oh days on 3rd Avenue,
Jane's acne, my work, nights of Byron, Larry's terrible addic-
tion, the virginity of John Ashbery and his going-home-early-
to-work evenings, an Afghan Hound named Zem-zem. 'Ah
dumb youth.' (—Leopardi)

FRANZ KLINE:
I understand everything you say. I like you because you're a:
skinny drink of water, handsome when you're alone, an imita-
tion of your monkey mask, a Mountain of Moles, a Matador
of Joy, a Fisher in the Sea of Mother Progress, a Stutterer
Who Improved, a green shirt with the collar turned, a Way of
Coming Closer, a Fawner in the Court of Jane, and mostly a
generous person especially with money, a Great Collector, in
short, art's got you by the balls.

KENNETH:
Abroad! a wonderful state! on the rue de l'Abbaye! Climbing
the Spanish Steps on your buttocks! while a gondolier you
know examines a road map of Rego Park! Canaletto was
good. A warm bed with a tall Swede, oh the masturbating into
a fjord of it all! The mists of Greece, I mean the hot suns
. . . through my glasses burning holes in my cheeks. Staring
at the Parthenon a glass of orange juice and sending that darling postcard to Jane with my hand in my hat.
    The village rats of Chartres. How I long for water where
women wash clothes. O soap! sponge! Lysol! fingernails imprisoned in lavender underdrawers, fish, albumen! A lift
from Dijon to Nice, a bearded Duke at my knee, guess what
he had on his wrist: a thin blue wasp to be suffocated by your
tongue. Ghiberti's gates could make one believe . . . Europe! Daddy! A strange thing happened in a bus:
    It was a very bright day in Florence. The sun was out. The
garlic was in bloom. I was hurrying out to Fiesole to see a
stone that a monk recently found in his bed when he woke up.
Knowing Landor died there made me feel quite cheerful
about the trip. I thought I'd first visit the cemetery and then

look at the stone. Would it be a transcendental experience? To continue. It was a long hot ride on a small trolley, the kind of trolley they only have in Italy. It costs so much to live. A woman was crying beside me. I asked her "What's wrong?" She said "Come home with me and find out." The cemetery only took ten minutes and the stone had already been purchased by the Detroit Art Institute. Her dark whimpers made up for it all. O nuns of Fiesole! The streets at seven o'clock were empty and cool as I walked slowly homeward with a novel by Raymond Queneau I'd borrowed from the convent library safely tucked under my arm. Stendhal was right when he called them a nation of brooders.

That was Italy for me. The next day I embarked for The Lowlands. Poland. Outside Krakow.

Dusk was falling on the marshes. A pair of flagging spirits flew by. Beneath a tree near a brook three soldiers were drunk and singing, "We're three, perhaps two, hellish fellows hailing from the flaming Donetz . . ." They invited me over, but I said "uh uh", remembering tales John Ashes had told me about rough trade. You don't have to be a queen to get beaten up. I couldn't restrain myself, however. I moved closer to them and said with all the courage I could muster, "Do you hate me?" They understood my tongue, those panis. In a few minutes I was as drunk as the best looking one. "Answer me!" I kept shouting, so they got up and threw me into the brook. Yes, the past is a hotel where all the rooms are a joy to behold. Why are the Swedish tall? Why are the Belgians interesting? Am I a negro? Is this literature? The lustful play of balding men, eating out their hearts over sandwiches, I am no bigger than their smallest. And is the purpose of life to be mighty in their eyes? Somewhere an egg is cooking. To be stronger than those whom you know are weak. Turn it over. Flapjacks. A room with a zoo. Oh eggplant! isn't it better to be John Myers than Waldemar Hansen? And isn't it marvellous that the A&P is already an institution?

Friends, past lovers, enemies of art, chefs, admirers of my poetry, bartenders and derelicts, cleaning women, enter the Travel Bureau of Beauty!

Foreign cities, the Catholic temples of God, the triptychs of Masaccio, the napkins of Matisse, the skies wherever they are

I forget, the fields where Michelangelo laid plans for David, let them creep creep into the hard unhoneyed parts of the heart, let them comfort you! 'Oh Frank, come away from the Museum of Modern Art, with your baked feet, oh Grace leave Walter, where are the autos of yesteryear. Oh John Ashbery you'll never be able to afford one, oh Larry Rivers leave fame to the Brachs, oh Bill de Kooning leave the Cedar, the Hessians are waiting, oh Jane Freilicher leave off, there is no colitis! oh Al Leslie behave yourself, oh Jimmy Schuyler why did you beat up Bill Weaver? Bill, forgive him! I am the snow-white Laundry Way. I am the Hand. Or Mouth. There is no intelligence, there is only Europe.

DE KOONING:
Yah, travel is okay, Poland, the marshes, it's terrific. It's like the signs I used to paint in Holland when I was a kit. Maybe inside the steeples it's dark, I don't know. But there's something about America that's further away. Take the hotdog for instance, it's simple and it's dumb and you eat it standing up. Cafes, talk, bah! Elaine was telling me there's this guy in New Jersey that made a lot of money, that's America for you . . .

A VOICE:
Hello. I'm Mark Rothko's mother.

DE KOONING:
Yah, that was the guy's name, Mark Rothko.

KENNETH:
I'm not talking about money, Bill. I mean that it stirs the imagination . . .

DE KOONING:
I only came out for a sandwich.

KENNETH:
Don't you understand me? There's a past and it's all there.

PAUL BRACH:
Here's your sandwich, Bill. But Kenneth, don't you realize

that New York is like Carthage after it was delended, that is, destroyed . . . And you know Dido showed at the Stable before she got upset. Well, that's art for you, and it's all in New York.

ELAINE DE K:
Bill, I just wahked bah youh stoodio un there wuz a kew of aht critics from Hoboken waiting to see youh wuhk. Whah duntcha go bahk un give em a peep, Bill. Bill. Bill, whah duntcha jump inta the Jaguah, it's outsahde, really it is. Nah don't cum dahn on yuh price, Bill, Giedion said youh great.

TOM HESS:
I've come to represent the American Renaissance, where is it?

JOHN MYERS:
Why, my dear, haven't you heard? I have a gallery of the liveliest, more original, and above all youngest, painters in America, and for every painter there's a poet. You know we've discovered something called "the Figure" that's exciting us enormously this season. I don't quite understand it myself but it has something terribly pertinent to do with the Past. It's called "Painting Divine" and includes the black laugh of surrealisme and the pile-strewn sobs of suprematism, and lots of boffing. Waldemar hates it.

CHORUS:
That's for us! (*Curtsies and bows and sings:*)
Curtsies and bows,
we are the nymphs of color.
Our hero wrinkles his brows
and returns to the attack. Duller.

KENNETH:
I was a Mason, boys. I come from an educated family. Though my grandpa dealt in burlap, my mother wrote up bridge parties for the Cincinnati Courier. Did you ever play golf? Have you ever seen a lawn? The difficulty was in being

Jewish. As a high school boy I was very interested in Zionism and changed my name from Cherrytree so I wouldn't embarrass the Jews. We parked our cars on the hill. The nights were simple. A soda. Thin girls in organdy. Where was the 14th century those evenings? Years later, necking in Chartres, I realized what we'd missed. I used to go and meditate in our oldest building which was built in 1938, it was so cool and restful. They called me "queer" and I thought they meant I was a poet, so I became a poet. What if I'd understood them? Moses! what a risk I was running. I know one thing about life today, I have my roots, just like anybody else.

(A bull enters the Cedar).

GEORGE:
What'll you have Jackson?

JACKSON POLLOCK:
Uh.

GEORGE:
Oh. The usual. Remember no cursing.

JACKSON POLLOCK:
Fuck you. *(Turning to KK)* My wife is a lousy lay, but you're the worst.

KENNETH:
You're a bald-headed idiot, and a perfect example of what I mean. America is very strong, but all it amounts to is action. You're about as necessary as an automatic salt shaker. But don't mistake me, I love your painting.

JACKSON POLLOCK:
Shit.

KENNETH:
How can we tell today? That's the tragedy, Jackson. I'm sorry I called you baldy. Were you serious about me?

MILTON RESNICK:
Your feelings are perfectly clear, but you're soft as a grape. Did you ever see those wops playing bocce under the David? It's turrible. Sittin in broken chairs near the tower!

KENNETH:
What tower?

MILTON:
The tower! you jerk. Listen. I knew a guy, pretty good painter. When he came back from Italy he was an inch. When I asked him what he thought of the Titians he said "You should see the Veroneses." I know it's marvellous and yuh feel like a grandson, you're a hero because yuh continue the battle, what good is terza rima, where do yuh fit it in, gimme an example, what good is Ariosto, Boccaccio, Delmonico, Guido, Longfellow, to you, you know you never write about anything but yoyos and brassieres and factories. Can yuh make a yoyo into sonnet? Movie stars are not Greek goddesses, I don't care if yuh stand on yuh head.

KENNETH:
The trouble with your argument, Milton, is that you're sentimental about not being sentimental. Do you think yoyo means simply yoyo. Come on, now. You wouldn't talk this way if Larry or Frank were here.

LEWITIN:
Those phonies.

JACKSON POLLOCK:
Those fags.

FRANZ KLINE:
Those dope addicts.

GEORGE:
Those cheapskates.
130

YVONNE THOMAS:
Dey are verry nice, I like dem verry much when dey're drunk.

MILTON:
What've they got to do with all this? They're nice guys, a little bit . . . but what the hell.

BILL DE K:
Yeah. But what were you saying, Milton. It was very interesting, what you were talking. It was a terrific point. Very mysterious.

MILTON:
Tradition, it's like a brick wall, you build it up, it gets higher and heavier every century but yuh keep going because yuh think there's plenty of room, and then it falls over on yuh. Why, in a hundred years nobody'll be able to do anything. And America, yuh know what America is? it's pushing that wall down. It's guys like you that're stoppin us. If I had my way I wouldn't let anybody go to Europe. You know what the New York School is? It's a lot of guys who know all about bricks. It's us. And listen to me. It may be a plain point of view but it's better than any I've heard in a long time. It's got vitality. We're pushin em down day and night. It's a cold water loft revolution. Take that Brooks Brothers look off your face. Put on these dungarees. Elaine broke em in herself.

ELAINE:
No, Milton. No. It was Kaldis. It was the last thing he did before he left.

CHORUS:
Wahhhh! Kaldis, oh oh oh, oh Kaldis, etc.

KENNETH:
I don't care if Gorky broke them in!

PHILIP PAVIA:
You WHAT!

131

KENNETH:

Yes, you fools. You think every time you step into an automobile you have to invent it. You think you're better than me because you haven't been to Europe. Well I got the Times every day while I was away and I didn't miss a thing. I smell the hot dogs on your breath but the poet in me speaks out. Yes, man is alone in this world and it's a good thing. It's like Prévert said "Oh Father who art in Heaven, stay there". I'm leaving, but not before I tell you what I think of you.

AD RHEINHARDT:

Philip. Why don't you get him for a panel at The Club?

KENNETH:

Greatness in art isn't heavy, it's light. It strains to leave the earth but it's light. Rubens' entire production is like a balloon, it makes me feel like a lark! You small men with big paintbrushes, you spend your days scaring little girls. You're just a bunch of housekeepers who sweep the ashes under the rug. Be brave enough to be disliked for being good, and sure. What do you care if you look like a Bendix? Don't throw your lack of talent into the wind! Spread it on a page. Let it say "I Love Florence!" Let it say "He is the illegitimate son of Rodin". Let it not just say, let it shout "I am the Masaccio on the bathroom wall".

(They knock him down, drag him outside, and tar and feather him.)

Act 2, scene

[Editors' note: play never completed.]

[UNTITLED]

A man dressed as Marlene Dietrich dressed as a man; the make-up should be reasonably similar but not grotesque, because the actor should not imitate her voice or mannerisms and should avoid camping.

Jenny in a short evening dress, plain and without jewelry, attractively modest most of the time but with outbreaks of temperament.

A sailor in a tight, dirty, rumpled uniform (enlisted).

Tarzan, one of the later ones, modern American style with no historical stuff.

Kenneth Koch.

Lydia [in manuscript, originally called Diana Powell, but changed by Frank O'Hara to Lydia, in certain speeches only], who must remain silent throughout. She is a "free" character for the director to do with what he pleases, including changing her role in the plot if desired or even making her heroine, since she is on-stage all the time.

MD *(enters and walks over to Diana)*:
May I?
(Diana looks vaguely at him and they begin to dance together slowly to something like "I'm in the mood for love.")

(Kenneth enters carrying Tarzan, if he can, and sets him down on his feet waving an arm toward him as if he were a sculptor and T. his work.)

KK:
There! you stand, the product of my genius, you might almost be my son. How lucky I am to have created something in the image of something. Darwin was wrong. You are not at all like an ape, you are more like a movie star.

TARZAN *(affably)*:
Thanks. *(Indicating loin-cloth:)*
This thing isn't much on looks, but it's very practical. You some sort of elephant hunter? *(suspiciously, but not menacing.)*

KK *(winningly)*:
No, no. I teach up at Columbia.

MD: *(over Diana's shoulder, friendly)*:
Hi!

KK AND TARZAN:
Hi.

KK:
It's not a bad job. We all have to make a living.

TARZAN:
That's what I was thinking.

KK:
Well, I mean, you can't just be a drifter and let the world take care of you. You've got to get out there and push . . . Well, you know what I mean.

TARZAN:
Yeah.

134

KK:
Besides, it keeps your mind clear, you keep working and
working and emptying out the old brain-pot. That way there's
room for a new idea every now and then. I don't like to
overdo that sort of thing, but when one comes along I like
to be ready for it.

*(Tarzan starts to cross toward MD and Diana and inadvertantly
nudges KK's shoulder.)*

TARZAN:
Ooops. Sorry.

KK *(furious)*:
Listen! It's all right to bump someone now and then, but
you've got no right to pull the rug out from under a guy!

TARZAN:
Go ahead. Talk.

KK:
Why don't you put some clothes on. *(insolent)*

TARZAN:
You're pretty fucking rude, you know?

KK:
You're no different from a third string quarterback to me.

TARZAN:
All you guys with glasses are like that. I don't care.

*(Diana disengages herself from MD, crosses and leans on Tarzan
with her arms around his neck, completely thoughtless, but comfortable. He pats her blonde hair. They dance slowly and casually.)*

MD *(to KK)*:
Oh well. Like to dance?

KK *(trying to figure him out)*:
Uh—I don't know.

MD:
What's bothering you?

KK:
I think I'm having a touch of H.D. all of a sudden.

MD:
H.D.!

KK:
Homosexual dread.

MD:
Curious kind of disease. Well, never mind. I want to get some chewing gum anyway. See you later.

(KK pulls out a little notebook and makes a notation thoughtfully until):

JENNY *(enters and crosses to him without paying attention to others)*:
Hello! I just had the most extraordinary experience. I saw a movie star!

KK:
Oh yes? who?

JENNY:
I think it was Shelly Winters.

TK:
That's nice. *Sailor enters and looks around)*.

JENNY:
Oh! there you are! here I am! *(to KK)* This is my brother Sonny. He's sort of upset.
136

SONNY:
I'm not your brother. I'm your husband.

KK:
I didn't know you were married.

JENNY:
I'm not.

SONNY:
Life is really awful, you know?

KK *(friendly)*:
I don't think you should take too harsh an attitude
about it. That's self-defeating. Give life a chance.
What could have happened to you that was all that bad?
I mean so much depends on how you look at things, how you
evaluate your experiences, and so on.

SONNY:
I can't evaluate them. I just stand and watch them go by;
and I don't like them.

JENNY *(to KK apologetically)*:
Something went wrong somewhere with that boy.

SONNY *(to KK mournfully)*:
She's unfair. Nothing went wrong with me, it was everything
else that went wrong. I'm holding my own, more or less.

MD *(enters again chewing, to KK)*:
Who's the sad sailor? *(to Sonny)* Want some gum?

SONNY: *(impatiently)*:
No, thanks. *(To KK)* You haven't got it straight yet.
I don't mind the atom bomb and diseases and accidents and
all that stuff. That doesn't bother me at all. It's just
that people are so god damned mean.

137

MD:
Hear! hear! why I remember when I made my first movie on the coast Josef von Sternberg was so damn . . .

KK *(eagerly to Sonny)*:
But don't you see it's your
attitude that makes you think so! Suppose you're walking along minding your own business and someone comes along and gives you a kick in the ass . . .

SONNY *(braking in)*:
That's exactly what's always happening!

KK:
. . . you've got to think of it as a love tap and keep smiling. Turn the dross into gold, boy, that's what I mean! Accept everything, and the world will lower its foot.

JENNY:
That smacks of Zen Buddhism. *(Tarzan and Lydia come over and listen.)*

KK:
No. No. No. It's plain old American Colonial common sense. Benjamin Franklin. Poor Richard. Walden. Isak Dinesen. Truman Capote.

TARZAN:
Stanley and Livingstone.

KK:
No. No. No. We had nothing to do with that. I wouldn't have such a clear conscience if we had.

TARZAN:
And what about the slaves?

138

KK:
Well, *I* didn't kidnap them, for Christ's sake. And I hope
you're not going to start in on the Indians, just when we're
getting to some positive statement that will help this
poor boy to adjust to life.

MD:
I think it's nice of him to worry about all those things.
How do you say it in your country? *injustices.*

JENNY:
It is nice of him, but where does it get you?

MD:
Where does it get you if you don't?

TARZAN:
I don't know what I'm doing here with all you creeps.

MD:
Oh have some chewing gum.

TARZAN:
That's another decadent attitude I don't like around
here. Why chew if you don't eat?

MD:
You really are remarkable. You don't have a nerve in your
whole body, I guess. I chew to keep from getting kind of
hysterical.

JENNY:
Why don't you chew tobacco?

MD:
It stains your teeth.

KK:
Well, to get back to the matter under discussion . . .

SONNY:
Nobody ever lets me talk. *(to MD)* You don't know what I
go through.

MD *(sympathetically)*:
No, I don't

JENNY:
Well, I do and I'm sick and tired of it.

KK:
What about art? what about poetry? Isn't it beautiful?

TARZAN:
I find poetry in simple things. *(to MD, helpfully)* Why don't
you take your clothes off.

MD: *(starts to take off jacket, tie etc., hesitantly)*:
You never know what you're going to find under all this
stuff. *(Takes off wig and is definitely a man now in shirt
and trousers, but still with high heels on.)* And it is
a relief to get down to brass tacks, so to speak. *(Kicks
off high heels.)* Wow! what a relief; I wonder what I thought
I was doing anyway. Modern life is so confusing! *(Formally,
as if making a debut, to Tarzan:)* Thanks a lot. *(to KK:)* Now
what was it you were saying that was so affirmative?

JENNY:
You didn't fool me for a minute. I thought you were attractive the minute I laid eyes on you.

MD:
Let's dance. *(to KK)* Don't go away, now. *(They dance.)*

SONNY: *(to KK)*
But I don't see what you've got to be cheerful about.

140

Tarzan:

I don't either. He has to get up in the morning and go
to that school or wherever, and teach a lot of uninterested
people, and stay up late at night in his hut grading papers, and earn money for little practical necessities such
as heat and food. I don't know how you stand it.

KK:

Gee, it is pretty depressing. *(Diana comes over and lays
her head on his shoulder comfortingly.)* How do I stand
it? Let me see: *(humming)* Hope springs eternal? . . . No,
that's not it. Into the breech, dear fr. . . Nope.

Tarzan:

Well, there'd be hope for you if you could face the rigors
of circumstance: fight a rhinoceros, tame a water buffalo,
get off your ass, man!

KK:

I guess you're right! Which way do we go?

Tarzan:

This-a-way. *(starting off triumphantly)*

KK:

Lead on! *(They exit, Jenny cries, Lydia seems to, MD comforts
them. Blackout for a moment. KK and Tarzan return and dance
with Lydia and Jenny: KK is taming Lydia patiently, mistaking her
for a water buffalo and Tarzan is combatting, or trying to, Jenny,
mistaking her for a rhinocerous, while she tries to get away from him,
then changes her mind and charges, etc. The sailor is in a spot talking to himself. MD has disappeared.)*

Sonny:

The war, after the strange mess of adolescence
which after all was worse than the war because I worried
so much about whether my pubic hair would really grow
and whether my penis would fall off if I . . .
but then the bombs were pretty worrisome too

because it's better to be alive and have no pubic hair
than to be dead with it, though I wouldn't go that far
with the other . . .
                    and of course it isn't really too different
I never knew where I was anyway, you look at the map
and say, Oh yes the Pacific Ocean, and later you think
for a minute and say, that's right the Colosseum is in
Columbus Circle, but what good does that do you?
                                              but I do
remember one or two places like lying on my belly
under a lilac bush once, that was sort of fun, and swinging
out over a lake on a rope and dropping off into the water
like that guy who was around here few minutes ago, who
was he anyway? he didn't look too sureof where he was either
someday I'll probably grow up and forget to wonder where I am
(looks into the lights)
hey! It looks as if the sun's come out and all's right with the world

(The stage brightens and the other four are arrested in their pos-
tures. MD enters authoritatively with a canvas bag over his shoul-
der and walks to the front, addressing Sonny.)

MD:
I've been thinking about things and I've decided that I
am the ideal person. I've thrown my gum away and I'm not
even nervous. I am the only person who can solve anything
around here and I'm going to do it. Why should I be self-
conscious about my natural superiority. Somebody's
got to do something. Specifically, I'm going to help
you. You may rescue one person and them I'll tell you what
I'm going to do.

(The sailor goes and extricates Lydia and brings her to the front of
the stage, the others remaining as they are.)

TARZAN:
Good. *(Takes two guns out of the bag and hands one to Sonny.*

They shoot the other three characters, who fall to the
floor without writhing or anything, like statues.) Now we
will make them into statues. *(They each take a body and stand it*
on its feet, immobile, at the back of the stage.
They come front and observe their work with satisfaction.)

TARZAN:
Now I have formed the New Republic. I have created a history
for you both and you will be bery happy. You are totally
useless and she is deaf and dumb. It is the perfect beginning. You have everything before you. I need only
give you one more thing and it will be perfect.
Guilt: indebtedness. And here it is. I shall go away. You
will remember me.

(EXITS)

SONNY:
What an optimistic type he was! But it's getting darker.
I wish there were someone else around.

(He walks away from Lydia and stands staring at the statues, back
to the audience, while Lydia crosses to MD, looks at him calmly,
then sits and places his head in her lap.)

MD:
I am sick and I am going to stay that way as an example
to the new society.

[Editors' note: Manuscript ends here.]

THE CORONATION MURDER MYSTERY

by Frank O'Hara, Kenneth Koch and John Ashbery

(for James Schuyler)

GIRL	Irma Hurley
MIKE	Michael Goldberg
PSYCHIATRIST	Kenneth Koch
JIMMY SCHUYLER	John Ashbery
THE BODY	Frank O'Hara
JOHN MYERS	Hal Fondren
JANE	Jane Freilicher
LARRY	Larry Rivers

Scene: Mike Goldberg's studio, 86 East 10th Street. At the opening, Jimmy Schuyler is visiting Mike and looking at his paintings when a pretty girl bursts in.

GIRL:
Forgive me for bursting in this way, Mr. Goldberg. But I need your help—desperately!

MIKE:
Get out of this house! No, no, don't leave . . . I just meant you were
standing in front of my favorite painting. *(She gets behind the painting.)*

PSYCHIATRIST *(entering):*
Pardon me, young man. I left my horse outside and I can't find it anywhere. Is it in your studio by any chance?

145

MIKE:
Get the hell out of my house! Are you a doctor? *(Psych. goes behind painting.)*

JIMMY:
Is that a new one, Mike? I like the way it moves up and down.

GIRL *(from behind):*
It's not the house—it's me. Who is this guy in here with me, anyhow? Oh, you're a salesman. Well, that's all right then. *(Pause.)*
Look, I need your help. My brother has been murdered. At least, I
think he was.

JOHN MYERS *(enters):*
I told Dore Ashton she ought to publish your new play, Larry.

JIMMY:
Gee, Mike, is Larry here too?

MIKE:
Larry's her brother.

JIMMY:
Oh, I'm sorry. What was his play about?

PSYCH *(coming out with Girl):*
John Button says that Hershey Bars melt if you keep them at room temperature.

GIRL:
Joan Mitchell says they don't. You can't tell who to believe. Meanwhile my brother . . .

JOHN MYERS:
Larry, I simply love that play.

146

GIRL:
Barbara Guest once bought this Milky Way in Italy . . .

MIKE:
Little does she know it, but there's another body back there
and it isn't her brother Larry's either.

JOHN MYERS:
Dore says it will be in the next issue.

GIRL:
John has this new Bessarabian poet he wants to publish who's
not as good as Jimmy's novel. He paints gravel poems!

JOHN MYERS:
Jimmy's novel isn't a person and you know it. And neither is
the Bessarabian, for that matter.

PSYCH:
Bessarabian! There was a strange odor of oil around your
brother!

JOHN MYERS:
Martha Jackson wants to punish the murderer, if he can be
found.

JIMMY:
I didn't know you had a brother, Mike.

PSYCH:
Let's get to the bottom of all these relationships.

JOHN MYERS:
The Buffalo Courier-Express gave it two columns.

MIKE:
If we can find out which house the murder was committed in,
we might have a very important clue.

GIRL:
Fairfield, would you pass me those Norman Bluhm playing cards, please.

JIMMY *(to Mike):*
I think you should call it "Watermill, August 13, 1955."

JOHN MYERS:
Elaine told me that if we ever find the real murderer, we will cease to mean anything to each other.

PSYCH:
Elaine told me just the opposite.

GIRL:
John Button says Arnold says we can all watch it on their set. Douglas Dumbrille plays Nietzsche, and Joan Leslie plays Clara Schumann.

MIKE:
Yes, Jimmy. I definitely think we should find the murderer and make friends with him. Norman says they're very popular in Paris.

PSYCH:
I would like to tell you all how I came by my jar of Jane Freilicher peanut butter.

GIRL:
Naomi wanted to have us over.

JANE *(from audience):*
You do, Doc, and you're a dead duck.

PSYCH:
I was standing at my window one bright Spring morning when suddenly the breeze wafted it into my hand. Joe Hazan said I ought to accept.

148

JOHN MYERS:
And then, Doctor, where did you hide the knife?

PSYCH:
The knife is in the peanut butter. Yak, yak.

JOHN MYERS:
Isn't [Kimon] awful? I told him the Bob Cornell Al Leslies
were the best thing since Julie Harris.

JANE *(from audience):*
But none of this explains the smell of Bessarabian oil around
the corpse.

LARRY *(enters):*
Truth is a beautiful and distant thing.

JOHN MYERS:
They're taking the Newport Jazz Festival to the Brussels
Worlds Fair. It's called Jimmy Schuyler.

MIKE:
Little did I know when I started out in life that it would
all end up at one point: habeas corpus.

LARRY:
Well, isn't anyone surprised to see me?

JANE *(from audience):*
Uh huh.

JOHN MYERS:
Oh Larry! There were all these Siamese here looking for you
just now. They want to do a feature story on you in *Angry
Penguins.*

LARRY:
I rode here on a silver stallion and was half blinded by
the light of its beauty.

149

GIRL:
I loved her "Aubrey Beardsley Paints a Picture" article.
But Fairfield said it was too long and had no meaning.

JOHN MYERS:
Say not so!

JIMMY:
Say not see-o-ho sea-o-ho.

GIRL:
John Myers recommended me for the Brussels Worlds Fair
Nobel Prize. I won this prize. King Hal Fondren the Tenth
of Sweden awarded me a solid gold Jimmy Schuyler. This
trophy now adorns my all-white living room.

PSYCH:
All white living room, hmmmm? I'm beginning to put two
and two together.

LARRY:
It seemed to me I had lost all sense of time and bodily
existence.

JANE *(from audience)*:
It was Frank O'Hara who first explained to me the difference
between silver and platinum.

JOHN MYERS:
I just can't stand paintings framed in metal. Give me a nice
soft muslin any day.

MIKE:
When I was a child I would run up the John Gruen steps and
a Jane Wilson sparrow would alight on my shoulder.

JOHN MYERS:
I punished the Paul Goodman flowers by planting them in *my*
garden.

150

GIRL:

After I came back from my triumph in Brussels I was sitting one night in my all-white apartment reading Cervantes' Exemplary Novels by the light of my Jimmy Schuyler Gold Statue Award, and I suddenly said to myself, "What the heck!" A large powdery blue figure slightly resembling Janice Elwood entered the room. It invited me to play cards and I found my hands were trembling. A flood of ice water began to stream out of the l Jimmy Schuyler statue. The powdery blue Janice Elwood figure walked slowly to the window.

(scream)

PSYCH:

Does *Swann's Way* come after *The Captive?* or does *The Bachelor Party* come in between? Hand me that pencil that has Alvin Novak's name on it in gold letters.

JIMMY:

Joan Mitchell is using it right now to do a crossword puzzle, but she'll be through in a minute.

MIKE:

We *have* to solve this murder.

GIRL:

The Isidore Fromm Foundation has just awarded me its Roberta Peters Award of 25 dollars and a trip to New Haven, but the letter begins, "Dear Jimmy Schuyler."

JOHN MYERS:

Oh good! In that case Joe LeSueur will be able to send your gold Jimmy Schuyler statuette to the Spoleto Festival, as he dearly wants to do.

LARRY:

Well, I guess I'll be going. *(Stays.)*

JOHN MYERS:

When *Carmina Burana* was first done at Lucerne . . .

151

PSYCH:
Personally, I don't care about murder. It's love *I* find sinister.

JIMMY:
At La-hoo-hoo- la-hoo-hoo sa-herne.

MIKE:
Have you seen last summer's *Bonacker*? William Blake has
two full pages.

BODY:
Where am I? Why, I'm in a house. And for about an hour
now I've heard a pretty girl talking about me. What bliss!

LARRY:
Would Rudolph and Edith Burckhardt and Edwin Denby
please
come up on stage?

MIKE *(slyly to Jimmy):*
I asked Brayton what you wanted for your book being published and he suggested the *Dragonfly Encyclopedia*, but I got
you this book of three-act plays instead.

BODY:
Jimmy, you'll be glad to know I have solved the murder. Nobody
was dead, I was just thinking. And who this young lady is
I haven't the faintest idea. As a matter of fact, you are
the only person I know in this whole row of houses.

LARRY:
This young lady is my sister. And who *you* may be, I do not
know.

GIRL *(to Body):*
I work with Jimmy at the Museum. Please drink some Elliot
Stein orange and grapefruit juice.

152

LARRY:
I am the second person who has failed to die during this
frightful crime. Thanks to this body, which I do not know
but strongly suspect is Kenneth Koch I have been saved from
the silver oblivion I mentioned earlier. The young lady my
sister is a fan of Jimmy Schuyler's, and I have only discom-
moded myself in this unseemly way in order to introduce her
to him. However, I now forget which one of you he is.

PSYCH:
How beautiful! This is Jimmy Schuyler. But now come to the
window. The John Ashbery petunias have begun to blossom.

JOHN MYERS:
Have you seen "The Bridge on the River Bob De Niro"? The
Kiesler sets are awful, but Jayne Mansfield is absolutely
marvellous!

GIRL:
The John Ashbery petunia is my favorite petunia! Jimmy,
I hope some day you will have a flower named after you.

PSYCH *(rushing to window):*
Look! all of Pennerton West County is coming to crown
Jimmy Schuyler with Nell Blaine hydrangeas. It is the
world's most truly beautiful evening.

MIKE:
Personally, Jim, I think you're better off with a lot
of gold statues of yourself.

THE END

LOVES LABOR,
an eclogue

First presented by the Living Theatre, New York City, 28 December 1959, directed by James Waring, music by John Herbert McDowell, set by Norman Bluhm, lighting by Nicola Cernevich, costume supervision by Remy Charlip, assistant director: Diane Di Prima; with the following cast:

SHEPHERD	Michael Arquette
SHEEP	Joan Baker, Phyllis Wax
VENUS	Valda Setterfield
IRISH FILM STAR	Viola Farber
NURSE	Susan Willis
ALSATIAN GUIDE	Timothy La Farge
CUB REPORTER	Vincent Warren
METTERNICH	Franklin Miller
JUNO	Sallie Dramlette
PARIS	Fred Herko
MINERVA	Susan Willis

A rocky pasture on the side of a mountain of lapis-lazuli, and below a gentle stream fringed with boskage. Morning dew.

SHEPHERD:
O famed of the ancients! how dare
you sweat in the glamorous sun?

How many gods are going a-haying
who might drop in like a big hummingbird? *(pause)*
It is night, I guess, and we are asleep.
Or are [we] looking after our sheep?
> I don't care.
> I can't see a thing,
> not even a big bird.
> The day is done.

VENUS:
Aren't we old-fashioned to be up and about?
I waken each morning with such a sense of the air!
which is my own faintly luminous skin
still snoring slightly, and aware of yesterday's scent. *(pause)*
My heart cries "It would be passionate to be there!"
and I feel like a greyhound, chic, trembling, thin,
reclining in a marvellous blue racing tent
while a policeman bears down fast on a dishonest tout.

SHEPHERD:
Here sheep, sheep, sheep.
Time to get up, my darlings!
You've had your 480 winks.

SHEEP:
baa baa

SENATOR:
And now you observe life, in the suburbs; don't you see
why reforms are necessary? I mean, new forms? Aren't you
glad we got up early and came to see them in their natural
state? *(pause)*
They are so delightful it would make one believe
that the oyster's "habitat" must be the pearl.

VISITORS *(in kimonas):*
Yes! No!

156

ALSATIAN GUIDE:
Has anyone any telegrams to send?

IRISH FILM STAR:
Well I declare! And is it Arcadia truly?

NURSE:
Yes, mum.

ALSATIAN GUIDE:
Your telegram, miss?

IRISH FILM STAR:
To James Actiun, Esquire, Hotel Zabaglione, Rochester
New York. Dear pot: Sam has signed me for the Princess,
p, r, i, n, c, e, s, s, as in potato, ranch, incest, navel,
caesarean, erupt, Sonia, sap, in "Tower Pot"—do you think
I can say the lines? Help me, my own. Love, (signed)
Mavourneen O'Sash. Have you got all that? Charge it to
Sam Goldwyn, Hollywood, USA.

CUB REPORTER:
And then?

VENUS:
I may not be wise, but I'm knowing. That's all I'm going
to say about the matter.

CUB REPORTER:
Aw Gee.

VENUS:
No, no.

SHEPHERD:
Don't be nervous, dears,
they're only tourists.

If you get disturbed
your lovely wool will go sour.

SHEEP:
baa, baa

CROWD:
Look! We're dancing. Isn't it the end?

METTERNICH:
Trains and tears, they all die but I
don't break. My death, my rage,
my hunting doesn't fill the air
with shrieks. I'm not a torrent.
I won't speak where I should.
No, I will come here secretly
to the Black Forest of the Heart,
and here when I speak you will believe
in me, for my voice is an Arcadian violin
which in the other world's despised
as ambition or pride. Near
these blue hills I could have lived
pure as flames, far from others, free of
their laborious envy and the gnats.

JUNO:
I seem a little grand for this meadow,
but I've paid them the compliment of over-dressing.
I wonder if Cecil Beaton is here with his gun?

2.
Minuet—enter Minerva

Scene Two: *The scene is bathed in the sublime hues of sunset. A
filet of sole is drying on the shore of the crimson Great Lake. The
mountain of lapis-lazuli is seen to be merely one eye of the goddess
Minerva.*

158

SHEPHERD:
What a terrible day it's been
for the flock! the dust!
the noise! it's incredible.
And all this horrid publicity.
Will it ever be cool again?

SHEEP:
O shut up, you big dope.

PARIS:
At last I have made my decision, yes,
I'm as nervous as a cat, what a dilemma!
I wonder if I offended anybody?

METTERNICH:
As in all such cases, the decision
was based on external factors,
for beauty, understanding and power
have their own climates where remorse
withers, and each act is perfect
and itself. Our crystalline Arcadia
is ended, our last refuge shattered,
soon we shall seem interesting
because the landscape is disgusting,
and we are rapidly becoming human.

VENUS:
His curiosity about suffering seemed innocent enough.

PARIS:
I am maligned! I meant nothing of what I said!

SHEPHERD:
Come now, beddy-bye. Daddy
wasn't kidding when he said
the day was ending. To bed, to bed.

PARIS:
But surely one thing is as good as another!

METTERNICH:
I shall go elsewhere.
and speak rather more plainly.

IRISH FILM STAR:
I shall be a great success.
Truly, I don't know anything.
I'm not even particularly unhappy.

MINERVA:
You have enlivened the situation,
Venus, by your decorative power,
but in introducing the outsider
you've set fire to your own purity,
and the palace of the gods.
You, and we, have become the whim
of love, whose momentary passion
is the painful memory of this serenity,
a gasp followed by a shower!

METTERNICH:
                    Alas!
We are already too old for the world
to love us. Yet, perhaps with make-up
and sour cream and waltzes, in Vienna . . .

MINERVA:
What do you see in my eyes?

PARIS:
I see the towers of Troy illuminated.

MINERVA:
And upon my breasts?

IRISH FILM STAR:
A neon net in which are imprisoned the stars!

MINERVA:
And between my thighs?

JUNO:
A sea of blood whose waves lash the shores
and promontories and the resort hotels of our youth.

METTERNICH:
The sheep are asleep, and Minerva
is closing her mighty eyes.
The day has become a destruction,
all things meretricious are precious
for variety is let loose upon the world.

(exeunt)

SHEPHERD:
Tomorrow I must seek
new pastures for my sheep.

161

ACT & PORTRAIT
Al Leslie Film

We walked [down] 14th Street. It was cold. Soft bombs are falling into hard Arctic palmtrees. We are softly bombing our insides, our tough skin will splinter, our shell will fall away. Birth of Venus, nobody's. My eyes were watering.

John the Baptist or John the Beloved? I was thinking about all of that. It was eight o'clock and Dorothea got the children ready for school. Miles wouldn't leave, I had to force him. We didn't want the children to see us playing children's games. At least I didn't, that's why I'm called Saint John. I always think of others, no matter what it ruins for me. All my friends have three children, endless Holy Trinities. The thing about children is you wonder why you have them. You wonder how you have them. Only women know, boom boom.

Miles really bugs me. He's like that shit that used to pinch me when I was a choir boy. I like him the same way. Dorothea isn't beautiful enough either. That's what all us FRINKS think about: BEAUTY. Nice soft decayed flesh, no hardons no tight nipples. No up no down, no sinking and no swimming. Rat-a-tat. She took the kids to school. I wonder if mine got there. So young and so uninteresting. Small animals have small problems. She met me in the cafeteria. Miles is still with her. He thinks the world is a mess. No messier than he. No Messiah than Him. She should be President. Dumb but willing. Coffee means a new day. I hate coffee. The poor man's water.

Dorothea cries a lot in the daytime. Argues at night. I didn't enjoy it. Miles pretended to. All she wants is attention.

How old was I when I realized I wouldn't enjoy anything any more? Anxiety is just another form of entertainment.

Negroes are religious. I am religious. Therefore I am a Negro. At least I am not "white."

We walked on and on, hating each other. The air was better in bed. Now my eyes hurt, I'm coughing and out of cigarettes. I looked at them on the corner of 23rd Street and Seventh Avenue. I wanted to lie down and be run over. It will come anyway. I didn't come, but it will. Miles did. Come. DIOS BENDIGA NUESTRA CASA. We looked at the Chelsea Hotel, it seemed to be damaged like everything else. Dios bendiga nuestra casa. Two nuns walked by, looking like lady wrestlers. I thought of my childhood and my dirty underwear. My socks.

Pollution isn't interesting, you can't even see it. I'm a sight queen, I guess. If you can't see it, it isn't there. Until it hits you. Boom.

I wonder where the land of the orange trees really is? Not Southern California, maybe Nome. Maybe Pittsburgh, maybe Nagasaki. Maybe Nome. I'm going down there in the sweet polluted twilight if the sun ever goes down and if they ever go away from my quiet walk along 14th Street and 7th Avenue and 23rd Street. Who are they anyway?

It's raining. It makes me feel sweaty like last night. I hate to feel sweaty. That's not sex, that's just amusement. Going to bed with Dorothea is like going to bed with a nun. She's just a pal, sexually, she doesn't feel anything about me or him, she just wants to be accommodating. We're all generalized, like mannequins. It's nobody's business what people do when they're alone. Everybody is always intruding. But it never makes any difference.

She thinks she's some sort of cornball Salome. I think she'd like to have my head. Her and her mother. A flashing bolt. I got on last night. On what? I'm retarded. Henry Chickenhawk.

Guys in black leather jackets give me the creeps. Who doesn't want to be Marlon? Except in that burning up store. The Living Theatre sure looks dead, yak. All those colored panes of glass, but no light coming through. Miles talks on and on. He thinks it's sexy. So does Dorothea I guess. Plain

164

talk for plain people. That's why you take a walk. They used to take walks to read. Monks in Cloisters, nuns in Bryant Park. Now we take walks to not talk. The air is nice. anyway. It's not Malibu but it's something.

There's something about nipples that disturbs me. Sometimes they stick out, sometimes they sink in. It's like guns. Sometimes you have the safety on, sometimes you have it off. Keep your powder dry. I wanted to go to chapel and hear my son sing some sort of cantata, but I couldn't pull myself together. At least he's going to a good school. But he'll be disappointed. He may as well start early.

Religion is very Gothic. I'm agin it. Fergit it. I get nervous enough around real living palpable pulsating smelling persons, without something coming over the horizon at me. And yet I do look up and I do see the sky. What is it? Why is it blue? Why is that truck driver driving a truck?

If she doesn't cut that out I'm going to paste her one. She is "Miss Urania, an American girl with a supple figure, sinewy legs, muscles of steel, arms of iron." If I hadn't read that, I wouldn't believe it. Yeah yeah. "He was seized with a definite desire to possess this woman, craving for her as an anaemic young girl will for some great, rough Hercules whose arms can crush her to a jelly in their embrace." I wish she'd crush Miles too. I forget most of it. "He had pictured the pretty American athlete to be as stolid and brutal as the strong man at a fair, but her stupidity alas! was purely feminine in its nature." That's the way it goes.

"I seek new perfumes, ampler blossoms (I mean bosoms), untired pleasures."

We got to Seventh Avenue and Greenwich. I got some cigarillos. Like St. Eulalia, I looked at the cruising fairies with compassion. I definitely think that sex should be allowed between consenting adults. The only question is how to become adult. Let them worry about that as long as they're let. Of course nobody wants to be alone, maybe they need the police like Negroes need Mississippi. Consent has nothing to do with it. You look around, and you can't find anything to consent to. All you can do is try to forget it.

165

Miles is now in Viet Nam. Brave stand. Where was he when the cop hit Julian Beck over the head? Where was I?

I bought a copy of the Psychedelic Review. Timothy Leary's in jail for transporting a few leaves over the Rio Grande, brown buttered river of my childhood. This proves that war makes more money than narcotics for our divine economy.

I thought Miles was coming and I hated him for it. Minor envy of someone else's spasm. Why am I not rich, grandiose failure that I am? When will we meet, she and I, the other woman from someone else's dreams, the bright one, the upset one, the full one, the contagious one? Whatever may happen, come come come.

We decided to walk all the way to the Plaza and visit the Oak Room. They were shocked by our appearance. We were shocked by their appearance. It was truly delightful. Afterwards we sang in Central Park to some nodding hackies. We felt young, though we are all over thirty-five and ineligible for aggression. We felt bored and defeated, because we only liked each other. Love is a many-splendored thing all right, that's what's wrong with it.

I remember the wafer on my tongue, and it sticking to the roof of my mouth. I thought I'd suffocate. Then that bitch of a bishop hit me across the face to prove my courage. Boy do I have plenty.

I have plenty of courage and plenty of cowardice and plenty of all the other things you have to have to be a modern man. But you haven't made me really sick yet. That's why I'n saying "That's all, folks."

FLIGHT 115
a play, or
Pas de Fumer sur la Piste

by Frank O'Hara and Bill Berkson

I think the happiest days of my life
were when I was going to a chiropractor
—isn't that the most depressing thing
you've ever heard?!

How pleasant it is to be above that tundra of clouds with you.
It's almost like John Ashbery's childhood all snowy and exciting with occasional footprints and a slush streak here and
there.

Yes, the solid bank of clouds is as reflective as John's eyes as
he stares out his window into the courtyard wondering if all
the stray cats have been fed.

Are you American? Have you ever been to Limoges? Haut-
rives? Tivoli? Oslo? Palazzo Farnese—it solved the palazzo
problem forever, you know.

Are you a movie star?

I'm with the AAU. You speak French, don't you?

Oui, alors, mais, je suis très desolée de la celebrité de M.
Pierre Boulez en Allemagne, ou il est apellé "le Dieu"—oui
c'est affreux! en allemagne on lui appelle "Der Gott"—c'est
une chose dégoutante, parce qu'il est un français, mais pas un
musicien français: soit le bon dieu vrai sauver l'âme de Claude

Achille Debussy! Meanwhile back at the ranch everyone is imitating his Marteau sans maître which is, incredibly enough, a setting of the maitre tres vivant de la poésie française actuelle, notre magicien de bouche, René Char. A horrible state of affairs! How much are you declaring for those shoes again?

Well, it comes to ninety Katanga sheckels. But let's keep quiet about it, shall we? These seats have ears.

La Boule est dans le Casino. Est-ce que ton cul est aidé de ton linge aux pins noirs? Fou, eh? Prends ton bouillabaise par le nez, leve tes yeux, et, grace a dieu, tu seras libres de toutes problemes de boulverser.

That's his collaboration with the french language. How you like, Harry?

Oh, Piña, Piña, Piña! Elle est si net comme un siffle! And now that you have that ring you can return to New York like Charlie Chaplin and make Uncle Fred happy. I can hardly wait to see the Teatro di Prima's version of our Up the Acropolis and Down the Gullet with Wendy Hiller playing Marc Antony. But to get back to Charlot, he says Jean Renoir is the greatest cineaste in the world. Do you believe it?

Who do you take me for, Eckermann? Ciassime di suo modo, right? I do agree that tea is terribly messy when you consider the glissance of sherry.

Il y a 700 ans peintre chinois sa vie à etudier les oiseaux.

There is something cruel about this water.

We are coming out of the clouds. Now I see you for the first time. Hello, Mrs. Sturnbach.

And over there is Heaven . . .

Le Prince de Monaco à son tour a glissé sur le banane de l'âme de la princesse.

Da damyata.

It's a very clear day over Goosebay.

For strings.

Now that I'm up in the air with you, how do I get down? Oh I was so afraid you'd go to sleep again! Sometimes I think you'll never wake up! So what if you do look like that Poussin—I want someone to talk to.

But something funny is going in and out of the wing.

It's a feather.

Yeah, listen, you didn't even know Elba when you saw it.

Well, I know enough to know that you didn't give me all the chewing gum that was given to us when we left America.

Hello St. Bridget . . . How's tricks?

In Rio they called me Mame .
In San Paolo it's just the same
But in Cuernavaca ay-ay me back-a
They called me a window pane

        So nude was I in Venise
        Senso skirt or chemise
        The the local police
        Dressed me in grease
        And slid me off the premise
        s ssssss ssssss ssssss ssssssss
        ay ay the fellahs
        when they're opening their umbrellas
                    etc.

169

Now listen, this is for people. Look at this mess! Even St. Bridget couldn't glue it back together.

Down down down down down went the itsy bitsy aircraft whilst comparing itself to a great big Rothko sky-dome which seemed to flourish over Earth that day.

It's very relaxing writing your name with your nose. Meanwhile the Green Mountains are drifting Lazily by like a Viera da Silva. We're slowing down. I don't like that. And the toilet is out of Schiaparelli. Still I keep calm, I keep writing my name in the air with my nose, and then I write your name with my nose, and then I put under it your "characteristic" flourish which has so often been admired on Traveller's Cheques, and we sit here relatively content, not quite knowing what is in store for one or both of us, or you or me, all that type kind of stuff. I'm so glad you're awake again so I don't have to listen to other people talk.

You're a spoiled brat, aren't you?

Uh huh. In the bathroom I went blind, in the sky I went deaf. I expect I'll go lame in the grave. That's life. Diseases are for living.

Somehow Narragansett Bay looks like a beer bottle, the Hudson like a racetrack, the East River like the jet stream. You are beginning to look more like an island, yourself, all those happy mudpies on your left flank!

Actually I almost cut my nose *off* in that bathroom when the plane started lurching Terra Funka. Which is even worse than going blind when you think of it. I mean you've got to *breathe* don't you? Oh well, I didn't mean to start an argument. Which do you prefer the Nuage or the Pergola?

Prexy's.

170

Down down down went the silent deaf dumb and blind airplane.

Back in Paris John is picking his afternoon nooky.

Oh I thought you were going to say nose and I was going to say he's lucky to have one.

And the big dumb speechless plane even backed up a few times.

Like the rodeo in the Misfits.

I don't like Prexy's at all, I'm not even sure I like English.

Bump bump bump went the wheels and seats and stewardesses of the poor helpless senseless airplane.

Between Frank Stella and Michael McClure what's the use of landing at all?

"and he stayed on with his hand holding mine/to the end of the line/to the end of the line/clang . . . clang . . . glang!"

LOVE ON THE HOOF

by Frank O'Hara and Frank Lima

Frank I
Frank II

Scene: *A bedroom with twin beds, a TV set and other things, a door and beyond a sitting room with a radio and other things. It's a loft, with windows either shuttered up or boarded up. The characters on screen are Frank I and Frank II. I is lying in bed furthest from door watching TV and reading. II is lying on couch in sitting room reading and listening to radio. Indian summer.*

II: I'm warning you leave me alone.

I: Do you know what time he needs me for publicity tomorrow?

II: For gods sake don't bring him over after. I pay my half of the rent.

I: He's your friend too.

II: But you're the one who's making money off him.

I: Oh read your book.

II: How do you know it's a book.

I: Who's buying the liquor this weekend?

II: Who's coming over?

I: John. That's all.

II: Huh.

I: Hey. Did you really get layed the other night?

II: No.

I: I didn't think so.

II: Up yours.

I: Well at least it's mine, and I'm big on taste.

II: Read your book.

I: I'm sitting on it.

II: What is it? The Fall of the Roman Empire?

Phone rings in bedroom. I picks it up and says:

I: Hello. (Shot of girl for one and only time.) I feel like Superman.

Shot to living room where II overhears and says:

II: Huh. (Continues to read.)

Back in bedroom:

I *(continuing)*: So I'm hungover. I know I have a great responsibility in this venture. What do you mean what was I doing in a place like that . . . I like Turkish baths when I'm drunk . . . Look—I don't question you about your job and your laboratory analysis. Anyhow, I don't think anybody'd let you in a pool room. No, I don't mean billiards. Have you had coffee yet? . . . You have a lot of nerve . . . What did you ever do for me that I didn't do for you? . . . For goodness sake do you think I buy the Sunday *Times* for noth-

174

ing? . . . I think you're being silly, now. Why? because I'm a miracle in your life, that's why . . . Well up yours too.

Back in living room, II *shouts:*
Stop quoting me! (*Phone rings in living room. Shot of other girl also close-up.*) Hello? Hi . . . No . . . Just reading and listening to a lot of drivel . . . Of course it's in the next room it couldn't very well be in this room, I was reading . . . Well if you feel that way why did you call me up in the first place? . . . You didn't get any message from *me* from your answering service . . . Who isn't glib is dead, baby . . . Well I am alive and I forgive you for your nervousness . . . Oh come on, now, there's nothing wrong with nervousness when you're in love . . . Who me? . . . Are you sure that was me who couldn't get a hardon? . . . How can you tell? . . .

Phone: I:
I: I was just reading the suppressed sequel to Fanny Hill . . . Don't disillusion me and I won't disillusion you . . .

Phone II:
II: What do you mean I jacked off before I came to see you. . . . I never jack off unless I *know* nothing's going to happen . . .

Phone I:
I: Let's keep available . . .

Phone II
II: . . . but you have no discretions by a window . . .

Phone I:
I: . . . I mean both of us! . . .

Phone II:
II: Oh shit! why should I always be the one to get it . . . (*Picks up phone and moves into other twin bed, making himself comfortable*)

175

Phone I:

I: Look baby, to begin with, I think it's too early in the game because I only met you last night. I think the whole thing is silly. Don't give me that . . . Sir Walter Raleigh has nothing to do with this . . . So what's wrong with bourbon . . . You got crapped out on martinis last night and you got sentimental about fucking and I wasn't about to take you home and go to the Bowery Follies . . .

Phone II:

II: . . . I didn't say I *don't* love you, I never said I *did* love you . . . there are no mice in this apartment, you must be hearing things . . .

Phone I:

I: . . . anyhow I think the whole thing is pretty boring . . . you're always talking about the Colony and the Pavillon—I worked there . . . Oh really, well you sounded pretty foolish . . .

Phone II: . . . the Civil War? . . . I don't give a fuck what you heard . . .

Phone I:

I: Look. You acted like a trick. I didn't. (*Hangs up.*)

Phone II:

II:Listen. Be glad I didn't knock you up. *If* I didn't. (*Hangs up.*) (*They look over and smile at each other. Then they reach towards each other and in embracing fall on the floor. Fade out.*)

C REVISITED, *or*
The True Legend of Carole Lombard

Ted Berrigan
Joe Brainard
Ron Padgett
Lorenz Gude
Rosalind Constable

Leo Lerman
Gregory Corso
Sandy Berrigan
Barry Goldwater
Allen Ginsberg
Pat Padgett

A butte or mesa in far-off Oklahoma. Ted Berrigan, Joe Brainard and Ron Padgett are plodding along in hush-puppies and mantillas.

TED:
Gee, Joe, these mantillas were a terrific idea. Sure keeps the sun off the back of your neck.

JOE:
I got them in Juarez when I was getting divorced . . .

TED:
Were you married already!?

JOE:
. . . from my schoolteacher.

RON:
Joe collects things. We in Tulsa call him "the Collector."

177

TED:
Nice name.

RON:
This (*including the vast expanse*) vast expanse is our inland sea, which you, as an Easterner, will doubtless appreciate a lot, though it's no ocean.

TED:
Oh I think it's terrific. I think that's what poetry should be, like sand.

RON:
You mean always shifting, drifting into hills and valleys, subverting and uniting, creating great dust bowls full of orchards and dead cattle, blowing into your eyes and blinding you, making every man his own tumble-weed?

TED:
Exactly.

JOE:
My favorite movie star is Carole Lombard, who's yours?

RON:
Then let's start a poetry magazine. If we have this terrific idea we should give it to the world, not bury it here in the magnificent waste.

TED:
I don't know . . . The gratuitous act has . . .

JOE:
Let's call it *C.* For Carole Lombard.

TED & RON:
Okay.

178

RON:
But if we are to enter public life we'd better get rid of these mantillas. People might think we are just three more fags who write.

TED AND JOE:
Certainly not! Olé!

(The curtain descends as they are burying the mantillas in the sand.)

Scene 2.

The apartment of Rosalind Constable. Mr. Lorenz Gude is sitting with Miss Constable over a bottle of champagne.

LG:
. . . and so, Miss Constable, I naturally wanted to discuss the venture with you before sending for these three young geniuses all the way from Tulsa to New York. Once arrived, they may never depart.

ROZ:
Send for them! Poetry is sand! Go with my blessing! *(LG exits.) The phone rings. It is Leo Lerman.)*

ROZ:
Hello

LL:
Hello, Roz. What are you doing?

ROZ:
Oh nothing.

LL:
Come on, Roz, what are you really doing?

Roz:

I'm just sitting here quietly, musing over a bottle of champagne.

LL:

Champagne? You're up to something, Roz.

Roz:

No I'm not. *(Suddenly angry:)* And you'll find that out sooner than you think! *(Click. Curtain.)*

Scene 3.

Ted Berrigan is having a solitary beer in the Cedar Bar. Enter Gregory Corso.

TED:

Gee it's nice to be here in the birthplace of Abstract Expressionism. This must be the most dignified place in New York, outside of Grant's Tomb.

GREG:

Hey Berrigan. How come you haven't asked me for anything for your new magazine *C*. I just wrote a great new poem called Cunt and I think it would be more appropriate in *C* than in *Fuck You.*

TED:

Sorry. You're not sandy enough.

GREG:

I'm as sandy as any fucking other poet in the world.

TED:

Not to me, you're not. I have seen the vast wastes of Tulsa.

(Gregory exits weeping. Curtain.)

180

Scene 4.

Ted and Sandy Berrigan are in bed. She is pregnant but cheerful.

TED:
. . . and then I said, Listen here my wife's name is Sandy. Get the fuck out of the Cedar or I'll ram my fist down your throat.

SANDY:
Oh darling!

TED:
You know you're the very spirit of poetry to me, baby.

SANDY:
I'll say. *(Curtain.)*

Scene 5.
The Super-Chief, Barry Goldwater's compartment, with BG and assorted aides. Allen Ginsberg enters.

GOLD:
What sort of camp is that? that beard?

GINS:
That's not a camp. I've been away.

GOLD:
Who hasn't? *(To aide:)* Get the poor fuck a drink of good old capitalistic cognac with some plain simple seltzer. That ought to stiffen him up.

GINS:
Tell me, Mr. Senator, with all due respects, is it true that you were thinking of taking the cure in Berchtesgaden this sum-

mer and your advisers called it off because to some people it might smell?

GOLD:
That's a lot of communist crap. To some people everything smells. Remember what Edith Sitlwell said about Dylan Thomas?

GINS:
She said that about *me,* you rat!

GOLD:
I stand corrected, and don't get abusive. There are ways of dealing with people like you. A woman isn't safe walking down the street with people like you let loose. Come November you may be wearing the shoe on the other ear, as dear dirty Dwight once said of Taft.

GINS:
I'm not wearing any shoes.

GOLD:
Ha ha.

GINS:
Who is this woman you're so worried about who likes to walk so much?

GOLD:
That woman, son, is your sister!

GINS:
It can't be. My sister is married to a Negro and stays in bed all the time.

GOLD:
No wonder you're the way you are.

(The train comes to a screeching halt in the middle of the Mojave Desert.)

GOLD:
Who the fuck's driving this train?

GINS:
Ted Berrigan and Joe Brainard, that's who. This is where
Tonto lost his underwear and they're helping him find it. *(En-
ter Ted and Joe.)*

TED:
Okay Allen, did you find anything?

GINS:
Not a trace.

JOE:
Here have a cigar. Have a Havana. *(Goldwater starts coughing
apoplectically)*

GOLD:
God damn it, I won't have that sort of thing going on in my
stateroom.

GINS:
Pretty modest of you not to take a whole car. *(Gold has pulled
out a handkerchief.)*

JOE:
Hey look at that. Around his nose! it's Tonto's underwear!

GINS:
Ah ha! He likes Indian shit!

GOLD:
Nonsense, boys. I found it at the Alamo when I gave that
speech proving *C* stands for Communist, as in Davy Crockett,
Coonskin Cap, and Carroway seeds.

JOE:
Take that! *(He socks him and all three flee into the desert. Curtain.)*

Scene 6.

The apartment of Ron and Pat Padgett. Joe Brainard is sitting with them drinking a coke.

PAT:
As a collector, I don't see why you got hung up on underwear.

JOE:
It's a long story, but we have to get the magazine out. Actually, we were slipping downstream towards *D* so I grabbed onto *U* which stands for underwear.

PAT:
Oh. I see. *(curtain).*

Scene 7.

Ted, Sandy, Ron, Pat and Joe are visiting the gardens at Versailles. It is late afternoon and they are very happy.

SANDY:
Gee, Ted. To think of it! *C* magazine got us here. I never thought it would turn into a Capitalist organ.

TED:
Sandy, watch your tongue.

SANDY:
Why?

RON:
That column over there reminds me of that thing Courbet pulled down in the Place de la Concorde to show he was with the revolution. You know *C* was also named after Courbet.

184

JOE:
It was in the Place Vendôme.

PAT:
Stop acting like an art student, Joe.

JOE:
Sorry. *(curtain)*

Scene 8.

[*Editors' note: play breaks off here.*]

THE GENERAL RETURNS FROM ONE PLACE TO ANOTHER

to Vincent Warren and to Warner Brothers and Taylor Mead

First produced by Present Stages at the Writer's Stage Theatre, New York City, 23 March 1964. It was directed by Jerry Benjamin, with the following cast:

THE GENERAL	Taylor Mead
AIDE #1 (BERT)	John Worden
AIDE #2 (EDGAR)	Jeffrey Reiss
MRS. FORBES	Vernoica Castang
GENERALISSIMO	
CHIANG KAI-SHEK	Loren Bivens
GENERALISSIMO	James Spruill
FRANCO	Yvette Hawkins
MME. CHIANG KAI-SHEK	Mari-Claire Charba
TIE SALESMAN	Glyn Turman
NATIVES AND CITIZENS	Joanne Hargarther, Susan Shawn, Jacque Lynn Colton, Mark Duffy, Marilyn Lee, Darnell Beatty, Bernard Johnson

SCENE I:

Scurvy, an island community famous in the last century largely for the betel nut craze of its inhabitants, which led to cannibalism.

187

They stand in a small group center, waving small paper replicas of the flag of their country. which is solid black. The GENERAL *enters almost nude but wearing galoshes and a toupee. For each scene thereafter, the* GENERAL *will enter with one more article of clothing added, decorations, etc.*

GENERAL *(saluting cheerfully):*
I'm on my way BACK!

NATIVES *(impassively):*
Hooray.
*(*GENERAL *crosses and exits discouraged.)*

SCENE 2:

A camp in the jungle. TWO AIDES *lounging about, rather sloppily dressed. Enter* GENERAL, *crosses to card table and examines some correspondence.*

GENERAL (MUSING):
There's something very wrong with the state of things . . . people's attitudes . . . . Something very wrong indeed.

1ST AIDE:
I'll say there is. I don't know what's gotten into people. And there isn't even a war on. It beats me.

2ND AIDE:
And nobody pays any attention to us. Here we are taking this long arduous trip, and not so much as a reporter has shown up for three weeks!

GENERAL:
Well, I know it. *(Turning)* And what about yourselves? You might at least come to attention or something.

AIDES (together):
We don't have to, we're out of uniform, aren't we?

GENERAL:
Oh never mind. Just get me a banana, one of you.

SCENE 3:

An inn on the outskirts. The GENERAL *is standing at the bar drinking, somewhat as if he were waiting for Sadie Thompson. He is not at all drunk.*

GENERAL:
Well, my good man?

BARTENDER:
Okay. *(Starts fixing another whiskey and soda.)*

GENERAL:
Bit brisk, the weather, for these parts, isn't it?

BARTENDER:
It's practically a cold wave, it must be down to 92 or 93 degrees.

GENERAL:
Yes, it makes a man feel vigorous when the temperature goes down.

BARTENDER:
If it goes down.

GENERAL:
Of course. Certainly it must go down first, that is *if* a man's going to feel vigorous.

BARTENDER:
Exactly.

GENERAL:
Hmmmm.

(A lady in organdy enters, with parasol and picture hat.).

BARTENDER:
Good afternoon, Mrs. Forbes. How are you feeling today?

MRS. FORBES:
Divine! It's this magnificent chill that's come upon us so suddenly.

BARTENDER:
Yes indeed. What'll it be?

MRS. FORBES:
A pink gin, I think, though it is early in the day for one.

GENERAL *(amiably)*:
It's never *too* early in the day.

MRS. FORBES:
I beg your pardon. I wish you solders had never discovered these islands.

GENERAL *(drawing himself up)*:
I wish you ladies had never discovered drink!

1ST AIDE *(in doorway)*:
General, the jeep is ready. *(Looking in):* Hey, who's the chick? Is she coming too?

GENERAL:
Shut up, you fool! *(To* BARTENDER): I seem to be a little short . . .

BARTENDER:
That's okay, General, it's on the island.
(They shake hands.)

GENERAL *(exiting)*:
Thank you. It's a fine establishment you have here.

MRS. FORBES *(calling after him as he exits)*:
You brute! (*To* BARTENDER): Who was that anyway?

BARTENDER:
I don't know. From his conversation he must be some kind
of . . . intellectual, I guess.

MRS. FORBES:
Oh . . . They don't last long out here, those sort of people.

SCENE 4:

*Outside the Opera House in Saigon, Late afternoon, only a very
few people about. A* TIE SALESMAN *enters with a little rack of ties
held aloft.*

TIE SALESMAN:
Little did I think I'd ever sell a *tie* to a General! Especially as I
never have any army regulation ties to sell because I'm afraid
of being accused of theft or Black Marketry. Nevertheless he
bought one of my finest just-before-sundown colored ties and
put it on on the spot. His aides were stupefied!

1ST CITIZEN:
What did he look like, this General?

TIE SALESMAN:
He was a big, grand-looking man. Looked as if he fitted his
rank, or station I believe they say in the Occident. Had lived

in Paris for six months once. *That* part was very interesting. He's out to explain why he's coming back. But the odd thing, the Chief of the Radio Station, who is another customer of mine, says he doesn't know who he is. I thought they might want to interview him, but no soap. Oh, that's another funny thing about it all. By the merest luck, I happened to have a tube of toothpaste on me, and he bought if for FIVE NEW FRANCS, which as you may know is 500 old ones. How's that for good fortune?

ALL CITIZENS ON STAGE:
MAGNIFICENT!

SCENE 5:

The observation platform (rear) of a train chugging through a pass. Seated on it smoking cigars with their feet up on the railing (they're in canvas chairs) are AIDES 1 & 2, *hereafter called* BERT *and* EDGAR. *They are more or less in uniform, but each has on a very loud tie.*

EDGAR:
Teriffic scenery, Bert. I hope old Smokey stays asleep so we can enjoy it for a while.

BERT:
I don't know whether it's worse worrying about him asleep or awake. I think he's flipping his lid. Edgar, honest I do.

EDGAR:
I don't think it's as serious as all that, Bert. He's always been peculiar. But I'm getting pretty tired of sending all those cables for permission to visit Chungking. What's he want to go to Chungking for?

BERT:
He doesn't. It's a nervous tic. He only wants to go to places

192

he's already been.
(MRS. FORBES *enters.*)

MRS. FORBES:
I beg your pardon. I didn't know the platform was occupied.
Do you suppose there'd be room for me to get a glimpse of
this magnificent view before night closes in?

EDGAR:
Say! Didn't I meet you in that bar in Borneo a couple of weeks
ago? You were wearing a big flimsy hat?

MRS. FORBES:
Why yes, young man, I thought you looked familiar! I think
I'd like some gin.

EDGAR *(leaping up):*
Yes, ma'am! Right away.
(Exits)

BERT:
My name is . . .

MRS. FORBES:
Oh never mind. We travelers seldom remember names, hardly even faces. I find that I remember forms more readily. You
know, temples, natives, that sort of thing. Isn't the landscape
of Nepal astounding?

BERT:
We were here before with the old man. It's nicer this time,
though.

MRS. FORBES:
The old man?

BERT:
Uh . . . our employer.

MRS. FORBES:
Poor boys! It's so terrible to work, when there's so much in the world to see, to enjoy!

BERT:
Yes, ma'am.

SCENE 6:

Singapore Airport. The GENERAL *is out on the field with two technicians taping an interview for the "Voice of America." He's wearing his tie, too. Behind them, a big airplane. The* GENERAL *carries a spray of orchids.*

GENERAL:
I'll tell you one thing, boys, the welcome . . . Are we shooting? I mean, are we getting it down?

1ST TECHNICIAN:
Not yet, sir.

2ND TECHNICIAN:
Now sir! Now she's taking!

GENERAL:
I'll tell you one thing, boys, the welcome, it's been magnificent here in ol' Sing. I mean half the world is asleep, a *good* half if my expereince is any measure, and I can assure you I haven't been conked out at the switch. But here in Singapore the sun is shining and they know who I am and they know I'm back. Well, I came back for that—so they'd know it. Know what this is? It's a spray of orchids given to yours truly by the sweetest little Eurasian girl you ever saw. That's respect for you— thought I was the Viceroy of India, as if India had a Viceroy any more. (It doesn't, does it?—better check that inch with Central Int.)

Anyhow, I'm not vain. The point is to come back, not to be recognized. Art's long, and conquered people are short. That's why they don't recognize me: THEY DON'T EVEN SEE ME!

But this experience, like (and I feel I can say this honestly and with full conviction—ugly word, that, conviction) . . . like all experiences, has been a wonderful one. It's given me a lot, and I think I've grown a lot from experiencing the particular experience I've been experiencing. It's a matter, I decided the other day in a rather drafty club car on the way from Djakarta, it's all a matter of handling. Let me give you a simple illustration of what I mean that everybody all over the world will get. Will understand.

We all know that it takes handling, *handling*, to get anything done, to get anywhere. Now let's take a simple example. Does anyone actually believe that if Marion Davies had been properly handled she wouldn't have been a bigger star than Norma Shearer? That's what I mean by handling. Handling is taking a poetic, no I'll go further, an *optimistic* view of reality—AND MAKING IT STICK. That girl had everything (Marion)—big blue eyes, a gorgeous chassis, a voice—good God, she made a movie with Bing Crosby, didn't she? And what did Norma have? Well, she was a good enough actress, even a pretty one: but she had a walleye. What happened, you'll ask, and I'll tell you, I've thought this out, I'm not like some Senator on the floor playing with his blocks: what happened is MISMANAGEMENT, or THE HANDLING WAS WRONG.

Now this problem is the most important one of our time and should be taken up with the U.N. It's at the root of what in the thirties used to be called "All Evil." Well, these are better times, but not *much* better, and the free peoples of the worlds had better take all of this into account when deciding the fate of all the free and unfree peoples of the world. I'm not going to go into the career of Louis B. Mayer in the latter connection right now, it's too upsetting.

Anyway, thanks boys, and wish me a happy voyage.

TECHNICIANS *(together):*
Gee, that was wonderful. Have a terrific climb, General.

GENERAL:
Onwards and backwards, boys!

(Salutes and exits into plane.)

SCENE 7:

A fashionable hat shop run by a Chinese woman. MRS. FORBES *is trying on hats.*

MRS. FORBES:
It's so sweet of those poor boys to do this for me! I think I'll take this one with all the feathers. I never go any place, so they couldn't possibly get crushed.

CHINESE WOMAN:
You are very wise, White Lady.

SCENE 8:

GENERALISSIMI CHIANG KAI-SHEK *and* FRANCO *seated in camp chairs outside a pup tent in the Spanish hills. Early morning; they are drinking coffee served by two orderlies.*

CHIANG:
I'm telling you he's becoming the scourge of the South Pacific! He's always nosing about, poking his way into other people's affairs, mumbling something sad about what it's like to "return." Well, who asked him to return?

FRANCO:
I guess that cover of *Newsweek* went to his head. But cheer up,

196

things are bad all over. We all have our troubles. Europe's no bed of roses.

CHIANG:
Well it's no bed of saffron, either. How would you like it if the Commies had control of Gibraltar?

FRANCO:
We'd rout them out, by God, that's what we'd do.

CHIANG:
Well don't look now, but . . .

SCENE 9:

The office of a Travel Agent. MRS. FORBES, *again in organdy but wearing her feathered hat this time, is being waited on by a* CLERK *while a* GOVERNMENT AGENT *in a Malayan turban stands by, curious but impassive.*

CLERK:
Perhaps these pamphlets will help you to decide, Mrs. . . . It was Mrs. Forbes, I believe?

MRS. FORBES:
Oh I've decided already, I've made up my mind. I want to go to Spain. I want to go to India first. I think I'd adore Hydera-bad. Then by a very slow freighter or something through the Indian Ocean, rounding I should hope that corner where that curious little place is, you know: Aden! Then through the Suez Canal, if they've got it working properly, and on by Tripoli, and Carthage, and the Kasbah—oh! it's so romantic, I don't know how I'll ever pay for it all! And then there I'll be, I'll hop off Gibraltar like a goat and land in SPAIN!

CLERK:
That is a delightful plan. Let me just go and check the route

and accommodations for you.
(Exits.)

GOVERNMENT AGENT:
Now that I know you are definitely planning to leave our country, I am able to tell you that you will not be allowed to leave our country. That is our way here. We never cause anyone any anxiety until they force us to. You could have gone on living peacefully here without ever knowing, but it is not our fault that you brought this unfortunate circumstance about. Your papers are not in order. That's why I've been shadowing you all through the streets and byways of our glorious city for these several weeks, to see what you're up to.

MRS. FORBES:
Well I must say that's flattering! You must have so many other things to do! . . . And as for the trip, not taking it will be better for my hat.

SCENE 10:

The GENERAL *walking about an extinguished campfire. Early morning. A pup tent in the rear with four feet sticking out of it.*

GENERAL:
Morning. Morning, and they haven't polished my shoes and they haven't gotten up and they haven't started the fire and they haven't made the coffee yet. The funny thing is that they're both broke from buying that strange woman all those presents. How dare they act this way to me?—not that I'm in any position to fire them. The lower orders have strange habits of independence, especially when in the direst of straits.

I think continually of the Naga tribesmen. What a strange and desperate desire is theirs.

To be independent—how ironic and how lovely! As if anyone could be! And if one were, immediately the others would

198

arrive and tear you down, exploit you, rape you, and murder you. "Self-determination!" What an odd sologan. One might as well have a slogan reading: "Impossible!" *(Shaking off the mood and growing furious:)* WAKE UP, YOU IRRESPONSI-BLE . . .!

SCENE 11:

Same scene. The two AIDES *are finishing preparing coffee over the campfire and* BERT *hands the* GENERAL *his cup.*

BERT:
Here you are, General. It sure takes a long time to make coffee in the tropics.

GENERAL:
It takes a long time to wake up, too.

EDGAR *(cheerfully)*:
It sure does, doesn't it?

GENERAL:
I didn't mean that as a compliment.

BERT:
It's been my experience of life that the most important people always wake up early.

EDGAR:
That's been my experience of life, too.

GENERAL *(flattered, finishing his coffee)*:
Thanks, boys. I think it's about time for my morning nap. *(They go off and come back and start setting up a camp cot downstage center.)*
That was very good coffee, boys. Worth waiting for.

AIDES:
Thanks, General. *(He lies down.)* Everything okay?

GENERAL:
Everything that could be.
(They exit. The lights go out and a film is flashed on the screen. It is Africa on the March and mainly depicts screaming hordes of Africans attacking various things, places, and people. Now and then the GENERAL moans in his sleep. The film switches to an apotheosis of the new, smiling Africa marching together in grand [1930s] style, then ends. After a moment the GENERAL awakens and rubs his eyes, then sits up and looks around.)

GENERAL *(In a horrified tone)*:
Well, it's not MUCH, but it's a hell of a lot better than being THERE!

SCENE 12:

A rather decrepit nightclub (native-style) on a small Pacific island. LUOA is singing "Moon of Manakura" in her best Dorothy Lamour manner, while the GENERAL is standing in the doorway. A self-conscious Chinese is standing beside him as if waiting for him to order a drink. MRS. FORBES is sitting at a table with BERT and EDGAR. Toward the end of the song, LUOA sings to the GENERAL, who looks away in embarrassment, only to encounter the gaze of MRS. FORBES (politely interested) and BERT and EDGAR (knowing). He leaves when MRS. FORBES smiles at him gaily.

BERT:
How do you like that, the old goat.

EDGAR:
I guess we caught him that time.

BERT:
I wonder how he found out about this place.

200

EDGAR:
It looked more like that singin' gal found out about him.

MRS. FORBES: *(not hearing them)*:
What a strange, forlorn face he has. It's rather tragic, I'd say.

BERT:
Not if you knew him.

MRS. FORBES:
No, no. There's a future in that face; it has a peculiar, lonely strength. A future, and a terrible, mysterious past.

EDGAR:
How about another drink, Mrs. Forbes?

MRS. FORBES *(coming out of it)*:
You said it.

SCENE 13:

The GENERAL *is in a field of flowers. There are palm trees in the background and a sign in Chinese characters. He wanders about, admiring and sniffing, but not picking. He muses.*

GENERAL:
Hmmmm. I wonder if that's a gilly flower or a carnation. Oh well, what matter? One knows so little. And here's that crazy orchid that always reminds me of a seed catalog. When the adventure ceases to be speculation and becomes WORK . . . THEN boredom sets in. Then boredom sits down and tells you all about your activities in gray, greasy tones, tones like the sky over London on an average day. But what do I have against the British? The sweet William is a pretty flower, so there *can't* be anything *wrong* with England, any more than there can be anything *wrong* with Java or Bali. Well, but there

201

may be something inherently wrong with any situation where beauty exists.

If it is true that the lily springs from the dung heap . . . then shouldn't we be offended by every place where beauty appears? Dung . . . animal dung, or the residue of our own human efforts? The question is vital. For if through our failures we can produce a beauty which has nothing to do with us, which is of a different nature from us, then that's pretty sinister. I mean, failure never produced a beautiful person, yet it might produce a beautiful flower . . . well, not a flower but a building, or a poem. For instance, the Taj Mahal is a failure—it doesn't house India's largest electrical corporation, does it, or the General Staff? No, no more than a poem give you any information. I detest poems. Yet I can't deny they exist; indeed it's often relaxing to just leaf through a book of them without paying attention, like walking through this field of flowers. I don't admire them, they're just *there*. . . . I don't even smell much of anything. Now if this were a dung heap, I'd certainly smell *something!*

Shit, I never admired beautiful things, anyway. Never had time for them, never found them useful. The tragedy of architecture is: the only truly useful thing a building can do is let itself be bombed. Or just fall apart. Look at Angkor Wat. Everything on the face of this earth stays around too long. Of course, flowers decay faster than most things; maybe that's why I like them. But I don't admire them; I simply observe the wisdom of their disappearing sooner than, say, trees. . . .

Never liked children, either. They hang around, they grow up, they go on and on, and as adults they even cause more trouble than as kids. And they create crowds and then you feel crowded in. No, it's not nice, all that stuff. At least the flowers are only knee-high, so you don't notice how many of *them* there are.

(Enter MRS. FORBES.*)*

MRS. FORBES *(noticing him after a moment)*:
Oh! I beg your pardon. I thought I heard people talking.

202

GENERAL:
No, I am alone.

MRS. FORBES:
Perhaps you wish to be alone.

GENERAL:
Not particularly. Anyhow, it's an impossibility. . . .
Anyhow, it's a public garden, so who am I to be alone in it?

MRS. FORBES:
I'm Mrs. Forbes.

GENERAL:
I'm a General.

MRS. FORBES:
Yes, I know. I am acquainted with your adjutants.

GENERAL:
They're my *aides*.

MRS. FORBES:
I beg your pardon. You're not a very cheerful person, are
you?

GENERAL:
At times. *(changing the subject)* What's that you're carrying?

MRS. FORBES:
It's the poems of Rupert Brooke.

GENERAL:
Can't abide the man. Or poetry either, for that matter.

MRS. FORBES *(shyly)*:
Then perhaps it's I who should be alone.

GENERAL *(crossly, but courteously):*
Very well, madame.
    (Exits.)

MRS. FORBES *(after a moment, mysteriously):*
Oh dear.

SCENE 14:

MRS. FORBES *being served coffee by a large Negro waiter in a sidewalk cafe.* BERT *and* EDGAR *and a girl enter.*

MRS. FORBES:
Boys! I think I'm in love!

EDGAR:
It's the heat, Mrs. Forbes, the Malaysian heat. This is Constance.

MRS. FORBES:
How do you do, Constance. I really do believe I am.

CONSTANCE *(observing her closely):*
I think you must be too, ducks.

BERT *(bundling them off):*
Let's get going. Here comes the rain!
    (Sound of tropical outburst.)

SCENE 15:

The lounge of a hotel, and the sound of rain outside. The same four are seated at table, and a waiter of Eurasian cast is taking orders.)

MRS. FORBES:
I think I've had enough coffee for today. *(turning to Constance:)* Now tell me, my dear, are you not the very girl we heard not long ago singing "Moon of Manakura"? Forgive me for my obtuseness.

CONSTANCE:
Yes, I am Luoa. . . .

BERT:
Yeah, we got her away from the General.
(MRS. FORBES *looks hurt.*)

CONSTANCE:
. . . I found early in my career that where American soldiers were concerned the name Constance was far more advantageous than Luoa, though I *am* rather dark for a Constance.

EDGAR:
No you're not.

MRS. FORBES *(bravely)*:
Apparently I forgot to tell you who I'm in love *with*. Well, it's the General. The General in a field of flowers.

EDGAR:
IMPOSSIBLE!

MRS. FORBES:
He was! HE ABSOLUTELY *was*! I never talked with him anywhere else! You know that.

BERT:
He means: it's impossible that you're in love with him.

MRS. FORBES:
OH! *(Suddenly beaming:)* I know. Isn't it divine? To think!

205

. . . In love again, me! In love again, and in love with a General again!

SCENE 16:

The hall of a marble palace. The GENERAL *up a few steps from* BERT *and* EDGAR, *whom he is addressing.*

GENERAL:
God, it's great to be back in Manila! You never thought I'd make it, did you?

BERT:
Er . . . Ah . . .

EDGAR:
Yes we did.

GENERAL:
No you didn't.

EDGAR:
Well we almost did.

GENERAL *(purposefully):*
Well, I don't give a damn whether you did or didn't. We're here anyway. And there's going to be a little reinstatement of discipline around here. You two have been lounging around the islands with your ladyfriends long enough. I want every square inch of marble in this palace shining like snow in the Arctic. Get some buckets and some brushes and some knee pads, and get to work for a change! That'll sweeten your tempers and take that smug look off your faces. Then when you're finished we'll have a little cloak-and-dagger maneuvers to keep you in training, *if* you can walk by then. *(They have come to attention as well as they can remember.)* Okay, dismissed.
(They exit.)

SCENE 17:

(Taiwan, a terrace and a Chinese rose arbor in which sit the GENER-
ALISSIMO *and* MME. CHIANG KAI-SHEK, *apparently reading aloud to
each other. The* GENERALISSIMO *interrupts her in the middle of the
sentence.* "But for a long time she remembered the plangent
sweetness of that far-off garden with a tenacity . . .")

GENERALISSIMO:
A what?

MADAME:
A tenacity.

GENERALISSIMO:
Oh . . . By the way, I received a report this morning from
our agent, Lin Foo.

MADAME:
Good heavens! The General's not coming our way, is he?

GENERALISSIMO:
No.

MADAME:
What a relief! House guests are all very well, but *he's* a far cry
from Mrs. Roosevelt.

GENERALISSIMO:
Don't worry your pretty little head about it. Still . . . it is odd
that he'd be in our neighborhood and then go all the way up
to the Philippines without bothering us at all. I'm afraid it
may mean that we've become rather déclassé, my dear.

MADAME:
Better déclassé than a nervous wreck.
(A few scattered sounds of bombing.)

207

GENERALISSIMO:
That's my girl.

MADAME:
How well I remember him at our commencement at Welles-ley. So young, so dashing—it seemed the world was at his feet.

GENERALISSIMO:
All well and good, but he didn't get to be a Generalissimo!

MADAME *(fondly)*:
No, just a General, poor thing.

GENERALISSIMO:
That's what comes of being born in the wrong place at the wrong time. I've always maintained that. It's Yin and Yang, I suppose.

MADAME *(seriously)*:
You are a very wise man.

GENERALISSIMO:
Thank you. I wish more people realized it. *(bursting out)* Hon-estly, if they don't stop that bombing, I'm going to . . . :

MADAME:
No, darling, don't upset yourself. It will stop. As you always say, "Yin and Yang."

GENERALISSIMO:
Well it better. *(changing his mood)* Yes, yes. Now let me read you this delicious bit from *Vanity Fair*.

MADAME:
Oh Please!

SCENE 18:

A neon sign blinking "TOKYO NIGHTS" off and on. CONSTANCE *and* MRS. FORBES *are drinking in the latter's hotel room.* MRS. FORBES *in a maribou peignoir,* CONSTANCE *in her singing costume.*

MRS. FORBES:
One thing I'll say for the Japanese, the liquor's cheaper here.

CONSTANCE:
I know, but I was really counting on that job. I'm telling you, when that night-club manager said that to me backstage I got so mad I could have spit.

MRS. FORBES *(surprised):*
Constance! You wouldn't have!

CONSTANCE:
I didn't. But I felt like it.

MRS. FORBES:
Life takes its toll of one, doesn't it?

CONSTANCE:
You know it's one of those situations which are so aggravating that all one's principles, all the niceties one has strived to maintain, just go up in smoke! I was flaming mad!

MRS. FORBES:
It does sound exciting.

CONSTANCE:
Oh he was plenty excited all right. I was as cold as a cobra. If I'd been a cobra I'd have given him a good bite on his fat finger.

MRS. FORBES:
Try to get your mind off it.

CONSTANCE:
Oh I can't. I wasn't brought up for a life like this. I wasn't *equipped* for it. It's one thing to walk out of the palm grove onto a little wooden platform and start singing—but *le monde chic* is too much for this little girl. You can have it.

MRS. FORBES:
No, dear. I have had it.

CONSTANCE:
You're a wonderful person!

MRS. FORBES:
No, I'm not. Not really.

CONSTANCE:
And so modest.

MRS. FORBES:
OH CUT IT OUT! (CONSTANCE *is abashed.*) Sorry, dear. You were reminding me of someone I once knew rather well.

CONSTANCE:
Oh . . . That can be painful. . . .

MRS. FORBES:
It's not that. . . . It's just that I miss the General so much.

CONSTANCE:
Poor baby. Say! I miss those boys an awful lot too. Why don't we fly up and see them? I'm broke, but if you could lend me the fare I'd pay you back when I get a job in Manila.

MRS. FORBES:
Oh dear. I really don't *have* enough. It was so expensive buying my way out of Bandung.

210

CONSTANCE:
Yeah. Oh it's silly for me to think of going anyway. I don't love them, I just like them.

MRS. FORBES:
And yet, when I think of his stern face above those nodding flowers, the very figure of a General before his troops . . . No, no. it would be too painful. And he's probably forgotten me already. . . . What am I saying! He never even knew me! How silly.

CONSTANCE:
We're probably better off here. And tomorrow I'm going to go out and get some money.

MRS. FORBES:
I wouldn't do *that*, dear, it ruins your looks. There must be another way.

SCENE 19:

An airport waiting room. A large sign says "SCHIZODROME— ROUTES EAST AND WEST." BERT *and* EDGAR *are disheveled and staring accusingly at the* GENERAL.

GENERAL *(shouting)*:
. . . AND FURTHERMORE, HOW DID I KNOW THEY WANTED THE DAMN PALACE BACK!

SCENE 20:

A village square in Borneo, surrounded by verdure and in the distance the deep blue hills of Borneo. The GENERAL *and* AIDES *walk on, as if taking a morning constitutional.*

GENERAL:
Back to Borneo. Little did I think that cry would ever strike a responsive chord in my breast.

BERT:
Yeah, Chief. We always kept bypassing Borneo before.

EDGAR:
We let the Aussies take it—but I think it's *nice*.
(A group of NATIVES *appear and salaam and carry on generally.)*

GENERAL:
Yes indeed, and here they know who a person *is*, too. *(to natives)* I'm back, you see.

NATIVES *(enthusiastically):*
Hooray!
(They exit.)

GENERAL:
Yes indeed. *(to* AIDES:*)* A charming lot.

BERT:
They've got no hard feelings.

EDGAR:
Why should they? We've never been here before.

GENERAL:
Yes indeed.

*(*MRS. FORBES *enters.)*

MRS. FORBES:
Well for heaven's sakes!

BERT AND EDGAR:
Hi, Mrs. Forbes!

GENERAL *(warily)*:
Good day to you. What are you doing here?

MRS. FORBES *(embarrassed)*:
Uhh . . .

BERT:
Yeah, Mrs. Forbes, what are you doing in this neck of the woods?

MRS. FORBES *(bravely)*:
I was . . . running away.

EDGAR *(solicitously)*:
You're not in any danger, are you?

BERT *(solicitously)*:
Who are you running away from?

MRS. FORBES *(delicatedly confused)*:
I guess . . . I was just running away . . . from life! Oh I think things can get pretty painful sometimes, don't you?

GENERAL *(reassured)*:
That sounds pretty silly to me. Running away from life!

MRS. FORBES *(sadly)*:
I suppose you're right.

EDGAR *(relieved)*:
So that's all it was! Say, what ever happened to Constance?

MRS. FORBES:
Oh I left *her* in Tokyo. She was frightfully busy.

BERT:
Busy doing what?

MRS. FORBES:
I don't know, just busy. Besides, I found out she's a spy for
Chiang Kai-shek. Can you imagine? Her real name is Lin Foo
and they hardly pay her a cent for all her spying, so she has to
keep busy on her own.

GENERAL:
Well that beats everything!

MRS. FORBES *(eager to have his attention)*:
You don't know the half of it! Would you believe it: they don't
even pay for her coded cablegrams with all the information.
The poor girl has to go out and hus . . . and *work* to pay for
them!

EDGAR:
It's despicable!

GENERAL:
Well, I don't like spies. Never had any use for them. *(looking
meaningfully at* MRS. FORBES;) I think it serves her right.

BERT *(aside to* EDGAR*)*:
Of course *he* called them *scouts*.

MRS. FORBES *(eagerly)*:
I'm sure that's the sensible way to look at it. But she's such a
lovely girl, except for that one fault.

GENERAL:
Yes, I suppose she is. *(genially and appealingly)* And a girl has
to earn a living, doesn't she?

MRS. FORBES:
Exactly. Oh General, you're so open! So fair!

GENERAL *(beaming)*:
I try to be; yes indeed, I do try to be.

214

MRS. FORBES *(afraid her infatuation is showing)*:
Well . . . I'd better be getting along and see to my luggage
and lodgings. I just popped off the plane and went out for a
stroll. . . . I suppose you military people call it recon-
noitering? . . . Ha ha ha . . .

GENERAL:
What? Not at all!
(To AIDES*:)*
You boys run along to the airport and pick up Mrs. Forbes's
luggage, then engage a room for her at our hotel.
(To MRS. FORBES*:)*
That will do, won't it?
(She nods. To AIDES *again:)*
Run along, now! Hop to it!
(They exit rapidly.)

Mrs. Forbes:
Oh thank you. You're awfully kind to look after me. I find
travel so confusing, though I do it all the time.

GENERAL:
Yes, yes. Of course you do. *(thinking for a moment, then offering
his arm.)*
Now . . . what say we take a little stroll through Borneo?
Who knows, we may find another field of flowers . . . and
this time we'll settle down and have a good long talk.
(The NATIVES *start entering again, inquisitively.)*
Would you enjoy that?

MRS. FORBES *(after a moment, incredulously)*:
Oh, I'd love it!

GENERAL *(after a moment, possessively)*:
Well come along then.
(He leads her off as:)

Natives *(severally)*:
HOORAY! HOORAY! HOORAY!

SCENE 21:

Same scene, and following quickly on the last. BERT *and* EDGAR *enter loaded down with luggage of a bizarre and heterogeneous nature, difficult to grasp. They are puffing with exertion, so there are short pauses as they struggle across.*

BERT:
Well . . . *something's* happening at last!

EDGAR *(gasping):*
Nobody else knows who he *is!*

NATIVES *(reappearing, very cheerful, dancing):*
GO HOME YANQUI!
*(*MRS. FORBES *rushes on distraught.)*

MRS. FORBES:
Oh God! the most awful thing has happened! *(She pauses hysterically. They drop all the bags.)* Oh and we were going to be so happy together, I know we were, and now this! . . . *(more quietly:)* We walked out into the field of flowers. Everything around was radiant with promise. My eyes were shining, his eyes were shining, my heart was pounding, his . . . *(Screams, then recovers.)* No, it couldn't have been his heart, it was his . . . his . . . lungs. I knew he was going to say, "I love you," when all of a sudden he got all choked up. At first I thought it was perfectly appropriate, you know. I slapped him on the back. Then he keeled over into the flowers and died. He couldn't get his breath! It was awful! It *is* awful!
(She staggers.)
I'm afraid I feel a little faint. . . .
(Two natives grab her as she collapses. BERT *and* EDGAR *rush to her side.)*

Bert:
God! he never did that before.

216

EDGAR:
Well of course not, you dope. You only *can* do that *once!*

BERT:
I mean he was never allergic to flowers. I guess it was psychosomatic!

EDGAR:
He was a great man, *too great* to be domesticated.

BERT:
I guess he *was* a great man *once.*

NATIVES *(not comprehending)*:
GO HOME YANQUI!

THE END

APPENDIX:
Documents

Above Edward St. John Gorey: *Set design for Try! Try!*, 1951, pen and ink sketch. Harvard Theatre Collection. Presented by the Poets' Theatre, Cambridge, Massachusetts, February 26, 1951. Directed by V.R. Lang, lighting by Nancy Ryan and Charles E. Eisitt, sets and costumes by Edward St. John Gorey and Alison Bishop, with Hugh Amory as stage manager.

Above right Larry Rivers: *Backdrop for Try! Try!*, 1952, pencil, crayon, charcoal, oil on paper over burlap, 99 3/8 by 118 1/8 inches. Collection the Museum of Modern Art, New York. Gift of Mr. and Mrs. André Emmerich.

Right Production photo of *Try! Try!*, presented by the Artists' Theatre, New York City, February 1953. Setting designed by Larry Rivers, music by John LaTouche, lighting by Mildred Jackson. Photo Walt Silver.

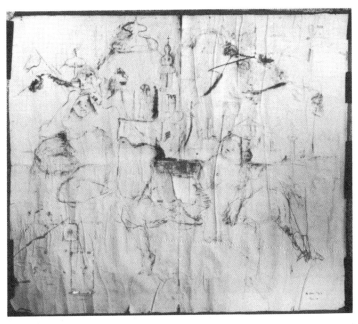

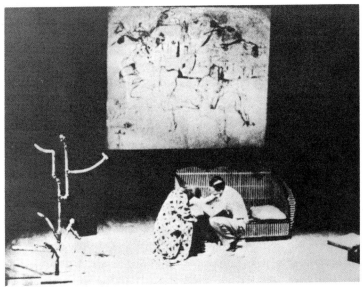

'Poets' Theater' Will Stage Plays Written in Verse

For the first time since George Pierce Baker took his famed dramatic workshop to Yale in 1925, undergraduate poets will have an opportunity to produce their verse-plays in the Harvard community.

A newly-formed Poets' Theater will present the first of five dramas on February 26, on the basis of "no admission fee, modest production, and all invited." Time and place for the production have not yet been determined.

W. Lyon Phelps '46, spokesman for the group, announced last night that the first program would be made up of four one-act plays: "Everyman," a masque by John Ashbery '50; "Interlude," by Richard Eberhart; "Try! Try!" by Francis O'Hara '50; and "A Play About Three Words," by Phelps. All of these poets have had poems published.

Working under the guidance of Professors Archibald MacLeish, Thornton Wilder, Harry T. Levin, and other faculty members, the group hopes to gain by practical experience a better working knowledge of the poet in terms of the theatre.

Future Possibilities

Phelps also pointed out that the work of all members of the community—undergraduates, graduate students, and faculty members—is welcomed by the organization.

"There is a possibility," Phelps said, "That this Poets' Theater could be the nucleus of a permanent adjunct to the American stage. We are starting on a small scale, and as we learn, the productions will become more polished, and they will also become more elaborate."

Above right Set design for *Change Your Bedding!*, produced by the Poets' Theatre, Cambridge, Massachusetts, in 1951.

Right Taylor Mead as the General in *The General Returns from One Place to Another*, first produced by Present Stages at the Writer's Stage Theatre on March 23, 1964. Directed by Jerry Benjamin.

220

```
........................the Poet's Theatre invites you to
a presentation of four one-act plays:
                ASHBERY      (Everyman)
                EBERHART     (Apparition)
                O'HARA       (Try! Try!)
                PHELPS       (3 Words in No Time)
        ..........to be given in the Christ Church Parish
House, 1 Garden Street, Cambridge, Mass.
Monday, February 26th, 1951.........................
```

THE POETS' THEATRE presents

EVERYMAN, a masque by John Ashbery

Columbine _____ Connaught O'Connell
Everyman _____ David Bowen
Death _____ Jerry Kohn

Music composed by Frank O'Hara

Piano _____ Rayna Klaizin
Flute _____ Howard Brown

THE APPARITION by Richard Eberhart

Robin, the host _____ Donald Hall
Berl, his wife _____ Renee Michaelson
Jason _____ Raymond Fitch
Wendy, his wife _____ Jean Liston
Charley _____ William Matchett
Grayce, his wife _____ Joan Rice

Directed by Mrs. DeWolf Howe

Intermission

TRY! TRY! a noh play, by Frank O'Hara

Violet _____ V. R. Lang
John, a friend
of the poet's _____ John Ashbery
Jack, Violet's
husband _____ Jack Rogers

Directed by V. R. Lang

222

The Harvard Crimson

The University Daily Newspaper — Founded 1873

Entered at the post office at Boston, Massachusetts, as second class mail matter December 1, 1877. Published daily, except Sundays, holidays, and during vacations (Dec. 22-Jan. 4; April 3-10, from September to May inclusive, five times weekly during reading periods (first two weeks in January and last two weeks in May) and thrice weekly during examination periods (last two weeks in January and first two weeks in June) by the Harvard Crimson.

14 Plympton St., Cambridge 38, Mass. Telephone Kirkland 7-2811. Subscription, per year, $7.00 delivered, $9.00 mailed.

Crimson Printing Co., 14 Plympton St., Cambridge 38, Mass.

William M. Simmons '52, President
Rudolph Kass '52, Managing Editor
William S. Holbrook III '52, Business Manager
David L. Ratner '52, Editorial Chairman
Marlowe A. Sigal '52, Photographic Chairman
Frank B. Gilbert '52, Associate Managing Editor
Edward J. Coughlin '52, Sports Editor
Robert L. Wiley, Jr. '52, Advertising Manager

Peter K. Solmssen '52 House Secretary
Herbert S. Meyers '52, City Editor
Roger Hahn '53, Circulation Manager
Humphrey Doermann '52, Assistant Editorial Chairman

Night Editor for this issue; Joseph P. Lorenz '53

Business Editor for this issue: Richard Rinderman '53

THURSDAY, MARCH 1, 1951

The Playgoer

Poets' Theatre

At Christ Church Parish House

Verse plays written and acted by students proved Monday night to have a surprising drawing power; a large and sympathetic audience attended the first evening of one-act plays by the Poets' Theatre. Although none of the works presented was completely satisfying, they showed considerable promise, and the reception should encourage future productions.

Most of the scripts suffered from beginner's errors in stagecraft. Few of the performers were actually called upon to perform; their parts required them mainly to recite monologues in formal poses. Little of the writing had really been adapted to the requirements of the stage. Nevertheless, the Theatre can be a valuable laboratory for these writers to improve their dramatic technique: particularly, they must learn to write lines meaningful and effective to an audience that hears them only once.

The first play, by John Ashbery, showed typical defects. The lines occasionally gave hints of being good verse, but not of the sort whose meaning is apparent at one hearing. However, the monologues were delivered with enough sincerity to make even dubious listeners suspend judgment.

"Try! Try!" by Frank O'Hara, was labeled on the program a "noh play," and we were handed some notes on the Noh plays of Japan: "The audience once dressed for them as if for a religious service in elaborate ceremonial robes . . . The audience is supposed to know all the plays by heart." Having put the modestly dressed audience on the defensive, the play earned the most appreciative reception of the evening. Violet Lang drew laughs with a number of dryly satirical lines.

Richard Eberhart's contribution, "The Apparition," was the weakest of the four, though it came closest to being a play. Unfortunately, it tried to be two plays, one within the other, all within fifteen minutes. Except for an amusing performance by Kay Levy the acting was choppy and hampered by a pointless script, the last part of which consisted of quite a lot of words in no particular order. Lyon Phelps' "3 Words in No Time" was the most complex of the plays, but despite careful staging and impressive delivery by Thayer David and Jerry Kilty, it was not entirely coherent.

One event marred the evening for some. Thornton Wilder, after an appeal for funds, lectured the audience vehemently on its "bad performance" during the O'Hara play, at which it had laughed loudly (and which got an extra curtain call). I think Mr. Wilder misjudged both the play and the audience's response; if so, his action was regrettable.

—Daniel Ellsberg

History

The Poets' Theatre was founded in 1950 when several of New England's outstanding poets joined forces with a group of younger writers in an effort to encourage poetic drama.

The newly acquired Workshop Theatre in Palmer Street was tested this past summer by the Poets' Theatre Acting Company with three productions by Yeats, Lorca and Middleton. In the previous season 1953-54, eight plays were performed, opening with two new plays by Archibald Mac-Leish, including This Music Crept By Me Upon the Waters, published as No. One of the Poets' Theatre series by the Harvard University Press. Yeats' Purgatory and The Player Queen were the classical revivals of the year. These were followed with plays by Rene Char, translated by Roger Shattuck, by Reuel Denney of Chicago and by Lyon Fhelps.

Two programs of short plays and one full-length play were produced during our first season in 1950-51. In 1951-52 we presented seven plays of varying lengths and a hilarious "Victorian Entertainment" directed by Edward Gorey in honor of our incorporation in the spring of that year.

Two outstanding productions of 1952-53 were V. R. Lang's Fire Exit, and William Alfred's Agamemnon. Fire Exit was revived by the the Artists' Theatre in New York last year, and Mr. Alfred's play will be produced on Broadway early next year.

To date, the Poets' Theatre has produced plays by William Alfred, Hugh Amory, John Ashbery, Rene Char, Cid Corman, Reuel Denney, Richard Eberhart, Paul Goodman, Edward Gorey, Donald Hall, Mary Howe, V. R. Lang, Alison Lurie, Frank O'Hara, Archibald MacLeish, Lyon Phelps, James Schuyler, Louis Simpson and W. B. Yeats. We have sponsored readings by some of these poets as well as by Dylan Thomas, John Malcolm Brinnin, Richard Wilbur, and Louise MacNeice. Mr. Thomas gave the first American reading of his play Under Milk Wood to a Poets' Theatre audience in the spring of 1953.

As an indirect result of our efforts, nine of our plays have been published, in magazine and book form, and are therefore available for production elsewhere. Others have been produced by groups in New York, Chicago, Boston, Seattle, San Francisco and in England. A list of those plays available may be obtained upon request.

1954-1955

Frank O'Hara was born in Baltimore, Maryland in 1926 and died in July 1966. He attended Harvard (B.A. 1950) and the University of Michigan (M.A. 1951), where he received the Hopwood Award in Poetry. He had published six books of poems—*A City Winter, Meditations in an Emergency, Second Avenue, Odes, Lunch Poems* and *Love Poems*—and a monograph *Jackson Pollock* (Braziller). From 1951 to 1966 he worked at the Museum of Modern Art, where he organized and prepared catalogues for exhibitions of New Spanish Painting and Sculpture, Franz Kline, Robert Motherwell, Reuben Nakian and David Smith. His *Collected Poems,* edited by Donald Allen and published posthumously, won the National Book Award.

Books by Frank O'Hara

A City Winter and Other Poems (Tibor de Nagy Gallery)
Oranges, 12 Pastorals (Tibor de Nagy Gallery)
Meditations in an Emergency (Grove Press)
Second Avenue (Totem Press/Corinth Books)
Odes (Tiber Press)
Lunch Poems (City Lights Books)
Love Poems (Tentative Title) (Tibor de Nagy Editions)
In Memory of My Feelings (The Museum of Modern Art)
The Collected Poems of Frank O'Hara (Alfred A. Knopf/The
    University of California Press at Berkeley)
The Selected Poems of Frank O'Hara (Alfred A. Knopf/Vintage)
Art Chronicles 1954-1966 (George Braziller)
Standing Still and Walking in New York (Grey Fox Press)
Poems Retrieved (Grey Fox Press)
Early Writing (Grey Fox Press)
Poems with lithographs by Willem deKooning (The Limited
    Editions Club)
Biotherm (for Bill Berkson) with lithographs by Jim Dine (Arion
Press)

Library of Congress Cataloging-in-Publication Data

O'Hara, Frank.
  [Selected plays]
  Amorous nightmares of delay : selected plays / Frank O'Hara.
    p.   cm.
  Originally published: Selected plays. New York : Full Court Press, 1978.
  ISBN 0-8018-5529-2 (alk. paper)
  I. Title.
PS3529.H28A6   1996
812´.54—dc20   96-38486
                                                   CIP